INDEX

FOREWORD

It was with great intrigue that I made the short journey from Alnwick to Embleton to meet the Rev. Michael Mountney late in 2004. Michael had contacted Alnwick District Council for assistance with promoting Embleton Church Council's "St. Oswald's Way".

Within days of this first meeting, it became clear that the St. Oswald's Way project had far more to offer Northumberland than the fledgling concept Michael and I discussed.

From that point, a year of hard work left the project in excellent health, with funding committed from Northumberland Strategic Partnership, Leader+, Northumberland Coast AONB and the four district councils along the proposed route. All of these partners must be thanked for their contributions towards the project in terms of both funding and expertise. Additional thanks are due to Northumberland County Council and the Northumberland National Park Authority for their technical support of the project.

November 2005 saw the appointment of the St. Oswald's Way Project Officer, Martin Paminter. Starting in December, Martin was soon up to full pace in an effort to meet extremely demanding funding deadlines. By August 2006, after months of hard work, St. Oswald's Way was open!

The efforts of the steering group, and not least Martin, had turned round a project in an amazing timescale. As Project Manager I must sincerely thank Martin, whose knowledge, ability and determination are really what made St. Oswald's Way possible.

The finished project of a fully waymarked route, excellent map pack, informative and interesting guidebook, and a variety of other merchandise have far exceeded the original vision. Hopefully, they will combine to provide a fantastic opportunity for people to enjoy for many years to come.

This leaves everyone involved in St. Oswald's Way happy to welcome walkers to our project. We sincerely hope that you find the experience rewarding and enjoyable as you follow a unique walk through some of Northumberland's finest landscapes.

Gary Campbell
Project Manager

St. Oswald's Way is a long-distance walking route, exploring some of the finest landscapes and fascinating history of Northumberland, England's northernmost county.

You will find castles, coastline, islands, scenic river valleys, hills, attractive villages, forest and farmland on your walk.

From Holy Island (Lindisfarne) in the north, St. Oswald's Way follows the stunning Northumberland coast, before heading inland across beautiful countryside to Heavenfield and Hadrian's Wall in the south, a distance of 97 miles (156km).

The route is based on a walk developed by the Embleton Church Council and links some of the places associated with St. Oswald, the king of Northumbria in the early 7th century, who played a major part in bringing Christianity to his people.

St. Oswald's Way is divided into six sections, from north to south:
Holy Island to Bamburgh (19 miles / 31 km)
Bamburgh to Craster (14 miles / 22 km)
Craster to Warkworth (13½ miles / 21½ km)
Warkworth to Rothbury (18 miles / 29 km)
Rothbury to Kirkwhelpington (15 miles / 24 km)
Kirkwhelpington to Heavenfield (17½ miles / 28½ km)

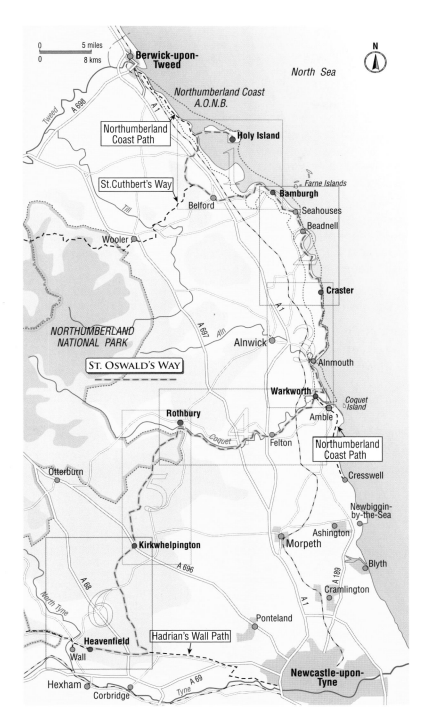

HOW TO USE THIS BOOK

This guidebook to St. Oswald's Way is full of useful information to make your walk as enjoyable as possible. General information and advice for the walker is included in the early part of the book, followed by the details of the route.

The Way is divided into six sections, from north to south, with distances of between 13½ miles (21½ km) and 19 miles (31 km). You can, of course, walk the route in different sections, or even in the opposite direction, but please be aware that the book is written from north to south.

Each section of St. Oswald's Way has its own chapter, with detailed maps and a route description to help you find your way. There is also information on the many interesting places and features to be found and numerous photographs of the beautiful views and historic sites than can be seen.

For those wishing to find out more about Northumberland, what to do, where to stay and how to get around, the final part of the book gives contact details for a number of organisations that will be pleased to help.

ST. OSWALD'S WAY CERTIFICATES

If you have walked the whole length of St. Oswald's Way, you will be able to receive a commemorative certificate. To apply for this, you must first buy the certificate pack, which includes a special rubbing sheet and a crayon.

As you follow the route, you will be able to find six St. Oswald's Way interpretation panels. Each of these panels has an individual 'rubbable' motif in the corner. Simply make a rubbing with the crayon onto the appropriate section of the sheet and, when you have collected all six rubbings, follow the instructions on the sheet to send off for your certificate.

The interpretation panels can be found at Holy Island, Bamburgh, Warkworth, Rothbury, Kirkwhelpington and Heavenfield.

A SHORT HISTORY OF OSWALD

St. Oswald's Way links three important sites associated with the Northumbrian king and saint, Oswald. These are the Holy Island of Lindisfarne, where he installed the first bishop; Bamburgh, which was his royal capital; and Heavenfield, where he camped before winning the famous battle that made him king.

Oswald was born in about 605 and was killed in 642. What is known of his life and achievements is almost entirely dependent on the 'Ecclesiastical History of the English People' written by the North East historian and scholar, the Venerable Bede, in about 730. This was some 90 years after Oswald's death. Bede portrays Oswald as a "man beloved of God" and the ideal Christian king – in life and death fighting for Christianity.

Oswald was the son of Aethelfrith, the King of Bernicia. Aethelfrith's wife, Acha, was from the royal family of the neighbouring kingdom of Deira, which allowed him to rule both areas in a joint kingdom known as Northumbria - that is eastern 'England' north of the Humber. Aethelfrith was killed by Acha's brother, Edwin, in 616 and Acha, Oswald and other companions fled to Dal Riada, in what is now Scotland. While he was there, Oswald was converted to Christianity by monks from the island of Iona.

Meanwhile, Edwin's reign brought peace and prosperity to Northumbria and he expanded his area of power westwards. However, in 633, he was killed in a battle against Cadwallon, the King of Gwynedd, and Penda of Mercia. Oswald's elder step-brother was king for a short period, until he was also killed by Cadwallon, who took a terrible revenge for the defeats of his people in earlier years.

Oswald had returned from exile when Edwin was killed and he marched south to Heavenfield to confront Cadwallon. Before the victorious battle, Oswald set up the standard of the holy cross before which, Bede says: "As far as we know, there was no symbol of the Christian faith, no church, and no altar erected anywhere in the land of Bernicia."

Shortly after becoming king, Oswald asked Iona for a spiritual leader to help in the conversion of Northumbria to Christianity. The first candidate was of "austere disposition" and soon returned to Iona, to be replaced by Aidan who became Bishop of Lindisfarne in 635. Lindisfarne became the cradle of Christianity in England.

Oswald ruled Northumbria for eight years and his reign ushered in a golden period in Northumbrian history in which scholarship, art and building flourished. It lasted until the Viking raids began in 793.

King Oswald went on to become one of the most important rulers in Britain but was killed in battle at Maserfield (thought to be near Oswestry in Shropshire), fighting his old enemies from Gwynedd and Mercia. After his death, his body was hacked to pieces and the head and arms fixed to stakes at the command of Penda.

King Penda

In the following year, the head and arms were rescued by Oswiu, Oswald's brother. The arms were taken to Bamburgh and, according to one source, Oswiu built the church of St. Peter at Bamburgh to house them. The head was given to the Lindisfarne Monastery, where it remained until the Viking raids forced the monks to leave the island in the 9th century. The head was one of the treasures, which also included the body of St. Cuthbert, that they took with them. Oswald's head is now in St. Cuthbert's tomb, in Durham Cathedral.

All these relics and the sites of Heavenfield and Maserfield became associated with miracles – and miraculous cures. These stories and the records of Bede were the beginnings of a cult of St. Oswald both here and on the continent. His life became the inspiration for legends as the cult spread throughout Europe in the Middle Ages. Stories and images of Oswald developed, in which a raven was shown as his companion and messenger. The raven is now used as the symbol for St. Oswald's Way.

PREPARATION FOR YOUR WALK

Before setting off on your walk along St. Oswald's Way, check the weather forecast and prepare yourself accordingly. Remember that weather conditions can change quickly at any time of year. Parts of the route cross remote countryside where it is always worth having proper walking boots and a set of good waterproofs with you, along with a first aid kit and enough food and drink. On the hills, it may also be worth taking a compass with you to help navigation.

THE COUNTRYSIDE CODE

- **Be safe – plan ahead and follow any signs**
  Even when going out locally, it's best to get the latest information about where and when you can go (for example, your rights to go onto some areas of open land may be restricted while work is carried out, for safety reasons or during breeding seasons). Follow advice and local signs, and be prepared for the unexpected.

- **Leave gates and property as you find them**
  Please respect the working life of the countryside, as our actions can affect people's livelihoods, our heritage, and the safety and welfare of animals and ourselves.

- **Protect plants and animals, and take your litter home**
  We have a responsibility to protect our countryside now and for future generations, so make sure you don't harm animals, birds, plants, or trees.

- **Keep your dog under close control**
  The countryside is a great place to exercise dogs, but it's every owner's duty to make sure their dog is not a danger or nuisance to farm animals, wildlife or other people.

- **Consider other people**
  Showing consideration and respect for other people makes the countryside a pleasant environment for everyone – at home, at work and at leisure.

WALKING ON ROADS

Although most of St. Oswald's Way follows public rights of way and other paths, there are numerous sections where country roads must be used. Please take great care when walking along roads and remember to follow the Highway Code:

- **Pavements or paths should be used if provided.**

- **If there is no pavement or path,** walk on the right-hand side of the road so that you can see oncoming traffic. You should take extra care and;

    be prepared to walk in single file, especially on narrow roads or in poor light,

    keep close to the side of the road.

    It is often safer to cross the road well before a sharp right-hand bend (so that oncoming traffic has a better chance of seeing you). Cross back after the bend.

- **Help other road users to see you.** Wear or carry something light coloured, bright or fluorescent in poor daylight conditions.

If you are a **large group** of people, you should use a path or pavement if available. If one is not available, you should keep to the left. Look-outs should be positioned at the front and back of the group, and they should wear fluorescent clothes in daylight and reflective clothes in the dark.

GOLF COURSES

The northern part of St. Oswald's Way crosses or runs alongside golf courses in a number of places. When walking through these areas, please follow the waymarks and do not stray from the path. Be aware of golfers and watch out for flying golf balls. It is not always easy to tell where the balls will be coming from, so keep a constant look-out as you walk.

OTHER LONG-DISTANCE WALKS IN THE AREA

St. Oswald's Way shares parts of the routes of other promoted walks that cross Northumberland.

St. Cuthbert's Way links a number of places associated with the former Bishop of Lindisfarne. It runs from Melrose Abbey in the Scottish Borders, crosses the rugged Cheviot Hills, then passes through Wooler and on to end at Holy Island. The route was opened in 1996 and is 62 miles (100 km) in length.

The **Northumberland Coast Path** is part of the North Sea Trail project. The Northumberland section of this pan-European route runs from Cresswell up to Berwick-upon-Tweed. It was launched in 2006 and includes the whole length of the Northumberland Coast Area of Outstanding Natural Beauty. The Path is 64 miles (103 km) long.

Hadrian's Wall Path is an 84-miles (140 km) coast-to-coast National Trail along the famous Roman frontier, from Wallsend in the east to Bowness-on-Solway in the west. It passes through some beautiful countryside, from rolling fields to rugged moorland, and includes the cities of Newcastle-upon-Tyne and Carlisle.

WAYMARKING AND SIGNAGE

St. Oswald's Way is, in parts, shared with other promoted walking routes that cross Northumberland. Although the route is waymarked and signed, we have tried to avoid cluttering the countryside with too many arrows and signs. There is, therefore, a variety of waymarking to follow as you progress along your walk.

 Public footpaths (yellow arrows) and public bridleways (blue arrows) are followed for most of St. Oswald's Way. Follow the waymarking for these paths where appropriate and look out for the additional waymarks and signs for the promoted routes.

 The first part of St. Oswald's Way, from Lindisfarne Priory on Holy Island to the mainland, is shared with St. Cuthbert's Way but is not waymarked. At the end of the Holy Island Causeway, the two routes join the Northumberland Coast Path. For the next few miles, the route is waymarked with the distinctive discs and signs for the Coast Path (featuring the symbol for the North Sea Trail), with some St. Cuthbert's Way signs too.

 St. Cuthbert's Way heads off via St. Cuthbert's Cave towards Wooler, while St. Oswald's Way and the Coast Path head south together. This part of the route is waymarked as the Coast Path as far as Warkworth (end of Section 3).

The Coast Path continues southwards down the coast from Warkworth, but St. Oswald's Way heads west along the Coquet valley (Section 4). From Warkworth you will see waymarks, logos and signposts for St. Oswald's Way, until beyond Great Whittington in Section 6.

The last part of Section 6 is shared with Hadrian's Wall Path, as it makes its way from east to west. The final few miles of St. Oswald's Way are, therefore, marked with the 'acorn' symbol used for all National Trails.

To help you, the maps in this book make clear which routes are shared in which sections.

PUBLIC TRANSPORT

Most parts of St. Oswald's Way can be reached easily by public transport. Using buses and trains is better for the environment than travelling by car, and you will also be helping to retain these services that are vital to many people in rural areas. If you cannot get to both ends of your walk by public transport, why not try using a bus or train in one direction and walking in the opposite direction?

Section 1 – Holy Island to Bamburgh

An irregular bus service runs between Holy Island and Berwick-upon-Tweed (where there is a railway station), also stopping on the A1 near Beal. Other buses run along the A1, stopping at Berwick, near Beal, near Fenwick, Belford and southwards via Alnwick and Morpeth through to Newcastle upon Tyne. Another bus route runs from Berwick along the A1 to Belford, then through Waren Mill and Bamburgh through to Beadnell.

Section 2 – Bamburgh to Craster

A regular bus service runs between Bamburgh and Alnwick, also stopping at North Sunderland, Seahouses, Beadnell, High Newton-by-the-Sea (occasionally) and Craster. Buses to Bamburgh and along the coast also run from Belford and Berwick-upon-Tweed.

Section 3 – Craster to Warkworth

A regular bus service runs between Bamburgh and Alnwick, also stopping at Craster, Howick and Longhoughton. Other buses link Alnwick to Longhoughton via Boulmer. An hourly bus service runs between Newcastle and Alnwick, including stops at Morpeth, Warkworth, Alnmouth village and Alnmouth railway station. Alnmouth railway station lies about one mile to the west of the village and just 1/2 mile from St. Oswald's Way. Trains to and from Newcastle, Morpeth, Acklington, Berwick-upon-Tweed and Edinburgh can be used.

Section 4 – Warkworth to Rothbury

Warkworth can be easily linked by bus to Alnwick, Morpeth and Newcastle. An hourly bus service runs between Newcastle and

Berwick, including stops at Morpeth, Felton and Alnwick. A regular service also runs between Morpeth and Rothbury, stopping on the A697 at Weldon Bridge (between Longhorsley and Longframlington) on the way. Acklington railway station is one mile from St. Oswald's Way. Occasional local trains stop here en route from Newcastle and Morpeth to Alnmouth.

Section 5 –
Rothbury to Kirkwhelpington
Public transport is fairly limited on this section of the walk. Rothbury can be easily reached by bus from Morpeth, with connections to Newcastle. Buses also run between Knowesgate, Kirkwhelpington and Newcastle.

© Northumberland Coast AONB
Gavin Duthie

Section 6 – Kirkwhelpington to Heavenfield
Public transport can be fairly limited on this section of the walk. Buses that run between Otterburn and Newcastle stop on the A696 at Kirkwhelpington. Great Whittington can be reached by bus from Newcastle or, occasionally, from Hexham. Unfortunately, there is no public transport to Heavenfield and no suitable car parking. You are advised to continue walking to either the village of Wall, or head south into Hexham. Regular buses run between Wall and Hexham, and it is also possible to get buses between Wall and Otterburn. There are frequent buses between Hexham and Newcastle, along with a regular train service.

The maps later on give a good indication of where you can catch buses and trains. Please be aware that routes are subject to change. For full and up-to-date route information and timetable details contact Traveline, whose details are at the back of the book on page 128.

CAR PARKING

There are car parks in various places along St. Oswald's Way, as shown on the maps in this book – please use these car parks where possible. If parking at other places on the route, please make sure that you do not obstruct roads or gateways.

ACCOMMODATION

There are guest houses and hotels at many places on the way, particularly along the coast (sections 1-3) and the Coquet valley (section 4). The countryside between Rothbury and Heavenfield, however, is quite remote and accommodation can be more difficult to find.

It is always advisable to book your accommodation, if needed, before you set out. Berwick-upon-Tweed Tourist Information Centre (see below for contact details) runs a '**Book A Bed Ahead**' Scheme for **St. Oswald's Way**.

You could also try the following websites:
www.visitnortheastengland.com
or **www.visitnorthumberland.com**
or contact the local tourist information centre.

TOURIST INFORMATION CENTRES

106 Marygate,
Berwick-upon-Tweed
Tel: 01289 330733
Email: tourism@berwick-upon-tweed.gov.uk

Seafield Road Car Park,
Seahouses
(seasonal only)
Tel: 01665 720884
Email: seahousesTIC@berwick-upon-tweed.gov.uk

Craster Car Park,
Craster (seasonal only)
Tel: 01665 576007
Email: crastertic@alnwick.gov.uk

2 The Shambles, **Alnwick**
Tel: 01665 511333
Email: alnwicktic@alnwick.gov.uk

Queen Street, **Amble**
(seasonal only)
Tel: 01665 712313
Email: ambletic@alnwick.gov.uk

Church Street, **Rothbury**
Tel: 01669 620887
Email: tic.rothbury@nnpa.org.uk

Fountain Cottage, Main Street,
Bellingham
Tel: 01434 220616
Email: bellinghamtic@btconnect.com

The Chantry, Bridge Street,
Morpeth
Tel: 01670 500700
Email: tourism@castlemorpeth.gov.uk

Wentworth Car Park, **Hexham**
Tel: 01434 652220
Email: hexham.tic@tynedale.gov.uk

KEY TO MAPS

Route information:

- – –🕊– – St. Oswald's Way
- – – – – – – Other path (bridleway, footpath)
- ⋯⋯⋯⋯ Track
- – = Gate, stile; footbridge
- ⚠ Caution - take care
- ☀ Viewpoint
- △ Summit
- ⛳ Golf course
- 🚐 Caravan site

Facilities:

- ℹ Tourist information
- 🚌 Bus
- ⇄ Railway station
- 🅿 Car parking
- WC Toilets
- ✉ Post Office
- 🍺 Pub
- 🍴 Cafe, restaurant
- 🛒 Shop

Features:

- 🏰 Castle
- ✝ Priory, church
- ☼ Archaeological site
- ⌐ Crag
- ᴠᴵᴵᴵᴵᵃ Sand dunes

Other long distance paths:

- ↯ Northumberland Coast Path
  (North Sea Trail)
- ✚ St Cuthbert's Way
- ⛫ Hadrian's Wall Path

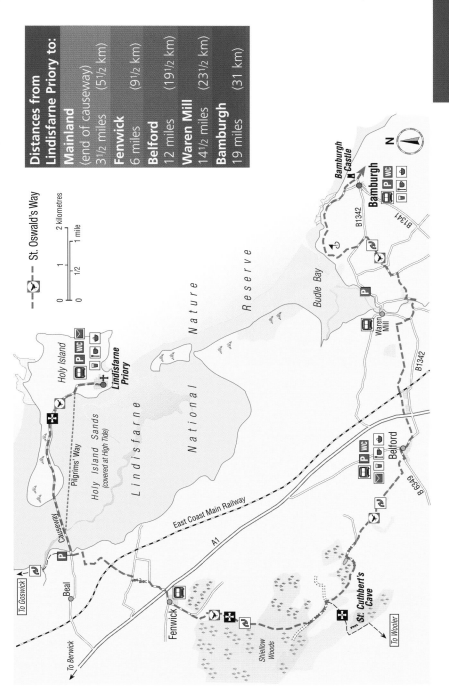

Distances from Lindisfarne Priory to:	
Mainland (end of causeway) 3½ miles	(5½ km)
Fenwick 6 miles	(9½ km)
Belford 12 miles	(19½ km)
Waren Mill 14½ miles	(23½ km)
Bamburgh 19 miles	(31 km)

--- St. Oswald's Way

Holy Island of Lindisfarne

St Aidan

The early history of Lindisfarne is associated with two bishops – St. Aidan and St. Cuthbert. Aidan was bishop until his death in 651 – about 16 years.

Of their monastery on the island, nothing remains other than what is displayed in the excellent Priory Museum. The monastery's most magnificent surviving achievement – the 7th century illuminated manuscript, the Lindisfarne Gospels, is in the British Library in London.

Lindisfarne Priory

The Anglo-Saxon monastery was attacked by the Vikings in 793 and these attacks continued until 875, when the monks moved to safety on the mainland. The monastery was re-founded as a priory in the late 11th century. The ruins that we see today include the priory's church of that time and later 13th century monastic buildings. The priory is now in the care of English Heritage.

Next to the priory is the parish church of St. Mary. This building is mainly of the 13th century – a restoration was carried out in 1860.

The other major building on Lindisfarne is the castle. It is built on a dramatic site on a rocky outcrop at the south east of the island. The original fort was constructed by the crown in about 1550 and continued in use until the early 19th century. In 1902, it was

bought by Edward Hudson, the founder of the magazine Country Life. Hudson commissioned the rising young architect Edwin Lutyens to convert the castle into a summer country home. This is the building we see today and it is now owned by the National Trust.

Lindisfarne Castle

1 From the start of St. Oswald's Way at Lindisfarne Priory, head towards the village, passing to the left of the stone cross. Go straight ahead then, at the road junction, straight on again. Pass the large car park on your right and follow the road down to Holy Island Sands.

Holy Island Causeway and Pilgrim's Way

Proposals to join the island permanently to the mainland began in the 1860s and were opposed by the islanders – a permanent railway branch line was also suggested at this time. The old route to Lindisfarne, the three-miles long Pilgrim's Way, is across the sands and is marked by long poles that were erected in 1987. The present causeway was completed in 1966.

The island remains inaccessible for a few hours either side of high tide. Stranded cars and passengers are still a feature of the causeway and were used to dramatic effect in Roman Polanski's 1966 film Cul-de-Sac.

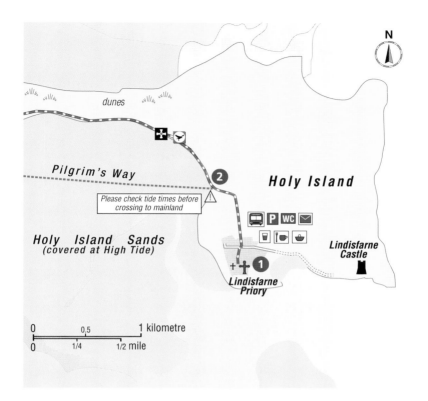

Holy Island

dunes

Pilgrim's Way

②

Please check tide times before crossing to mainland

Holy Island Sands
(covered at High Tide)

Lindisfarne Castle

+ + ① Lindisfarne Priory

| 0 | | 0.5 | | 1 kilometre |
| 0 | | 1/4 | | 1/2 mile |

② St. Oswald's Way follows the road and causeway across to the mainland. It is also possible to follow the Pilgrims' Way across the Sands, along the line of wooden poles straight ahead. Please note that both these routes are only passable when the tide is out and the Pilgrims' Way, in particular, can be hazardous. You must ensure that you have enough time to complete your crossing before setting off: check tide tables or a local tourist information centre for more information.

Pilgrim's Way

3 After reaching the mainland, turn left along the path opposite the car park. From this point St. Oswald's Way (and St. Cuthbert's Way) join the Northumberland Coast Path: follow the distinctive waymarking and signposts for the Coast Path, featuring the symbol for the North Sea Trail.

After 300 yards, the route turns right through a gate into a field. Follow the path ahead to reach a track.

Lindisfarne National Nature Reserve

The sands and dunes of Holy Island are part of the Lindisfarne National Nature Reserve. Tidal mudflats, saltmarshes and dunes combine to create a place that is home to fascinating plants and to a food supply that attracts bird visitors from thousands of

Bar-tailed godwit
© Tim Zurowski

miles away. The Reserve protects a long stretch of coast, as far south as Budle Bay.

Six internationally important species of wildfowl and wading birds spend the winter here, including the bar-tailed godwit and pale-bellied brent geese from Spitzbergen in Arctic Norway.

Lindisfarne also has international recognition – it is a 'Ramsar site', a wetland of international significance.

4 Turn left along the track to reach a field. Bear left across to the far corner of the field. Cross the bridge over the stream and follow the path ahead. Take great care when crossing the East Coast main railway as high-speed trains frequently pass this point. Follow the field-edge path uphill to meet a lane.

0   0.5   1 kilometre
0   1/4   1/2 mile

N

To Goswick

The Snook

Causeway

Pilgrim's Way

P

3 ⚠ Please check tide times before
crossing to Holy Island

4

Holy Island Sands
(covered at High Tide)

Lindisfarne

National

Nature

Reserve

⚠ Rail crossing-
high speed trains

5

5 Turn right, then left along the first track. Follow the winding track through to another lane. Turn right and continue past Fenwick Granary to reach the A1 main road.

The Great North Road

The 'premier highway in Britain' originated in roman roads and ancient tracks. However, as a through route, it could be said to date from 1603 when King James I (of England) instituted a postal service from London to Berwick. The Northumberland part of the Great North Road probably began as tracks linking the main towns of Newcastle, Morpeth, Alnwick and Berwick. St. Oswald's Way crosses the old route three times at Fenwick (where it is also the present A1), Belford and Felton.

6 Cross the A1 with care and go straight ahead into the village of Fenwick. At the first road junction, turn left and follow this road up the hill to another junction. Go straight ahead on the more minor road, rather than bearing left.

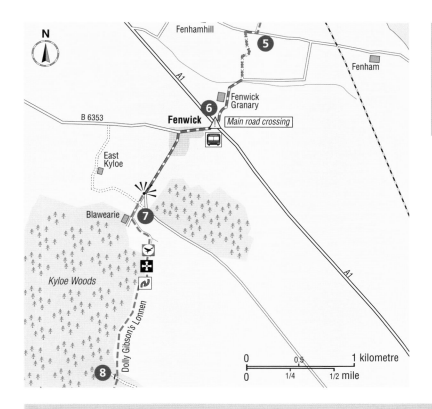

Fenwick

Fenwick today is a hamlet with a small number of houses – its shops and school have disappeared. It was originally part of the Haggerston Estate and the houses were occupied by estate workers. The present day village hall was originally a granary. It later became a reading room where the men of the village could play billiards and read the papers. Access to the upper floor is by external stone steps.

7 Just before the house on the right (Blawearie), turn left and follow the path along the field edges. With Kyloe Woods on your right hand side, continue along the path. The route joins the course of an old lane known as Dolly Gibson's Lonnen and enters Shiellow Woods.

Kyloe Woods

Red squirrel
© Keith Naylor

The woods were also part of the Haggerston Estate and it was here that Leylandii cypresses were first raised. The tree is a cross of two North American species that were growing close together in a tree collection at Leighton Hall, Powys in 1888. They are named after Captain C J Leyland, the owner of Haggerston, who took some of the seedlings from Leighton Hall (owned by his brother-in-law) and planted them here.

Kyloe Woods are now designated as a Red Squirrel Reserve. Britain's native squirrels are now missing from most of the country and these reserves have been set up to protect the local populations of these endangered animals.

8 Go straight ahead on the waymarked footpath through the trees. Cross a forestry track and follow the footpath to join another track. Follow the track straight ahead to a T-junction. Turn left on a public bridleway and follow the track out of the woods. Continue along the

track with Greensheen Hill over to your right. To the left are lovely views of the coast, including Holy Island and Lindisfarne Castle, the Farne Islands and Bamburgh Castle.

9 At a gate on the right, turn right into a field. Here, St. Oswald's Way continues with the Northumberland Coast Path, while St. Cuthbert's Way heads off to the right on a bridleway to St. Cuthbert's Cave (which is about 1/2 mile away and makes an interesting side trip). Follow the main path through the field, keeping the crags to your left, and into more forestry. Follow the main track, past Swinhoe Lakes and on to Swinhoe Farm.

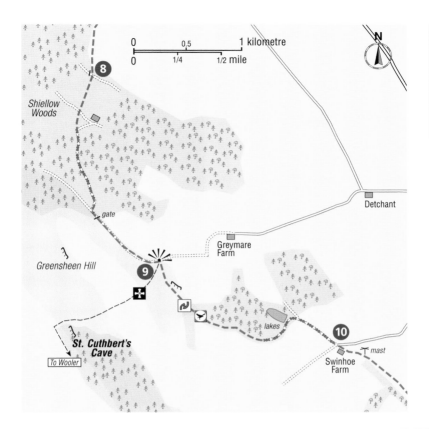

0 0.5 1 kilometre
0 1/4 1/2 mile
N

Shiellow Woods

Detchant

gate

Greymare Farm

Greensheen Hill

St. Cuthbert's Cave
To Wooler

lakes

mast

Swinhoe Farm

St. Cuthbert's Cave

When the monks of Lindisfarne fled from Viking attacks in 875, they took the sacred remains of St. Cuthbert with them. Legend has it that this scenic natural sandstone overhang was one of the places that they stopped. Other stories suggest that, when alive, Cuthbert used the cave as a hermitage.

Tony Derbyshire - Northumberland County Council

10 At the farm, cross the lane and walk between the buildings, up to a gateway into a field. Walk up the field and around the crag to a mast. Cross the stile at the mast and turn right. Follow the path around the tops of the fields, with Sunnyside Crags over to your left and woodland on your right. At the corner of the wood, cross the stile and bear left. Follow the path across the field and down to reach a track.

Westhall

11 Go straight ahead along field-edge paths, turning left and then along the right-hand side of a stream to reach a lane. Turn right and follow the lane to a road. Turn left and head into the village of Belford.

Belford area

Just before Belford lies Westhall farmhouse, a square, castellated building, built in the gothic style in 1837.

Belford developed as a post town in which, before the coming of the railway, the Blue Bell was a thriving coaching inn. The inn remains at the centre of the town close to St. Mary's Church. Although the church retains a Norman chancel arch, the building today largely dates from the rebuilding, by the well-known Newcastle architect John Dobson, in 1829.

Belford retains much of its character and former importance as a market town. The 18th century mansion house, Belford Hall, is set in parkland to the north-east of the church.

The crop drying and storage site to the east of the A1 is owned by Coastal Grains Ltd. This is a co-operative set up in 1982 by a group of 10 farmers, although there are now many more members.

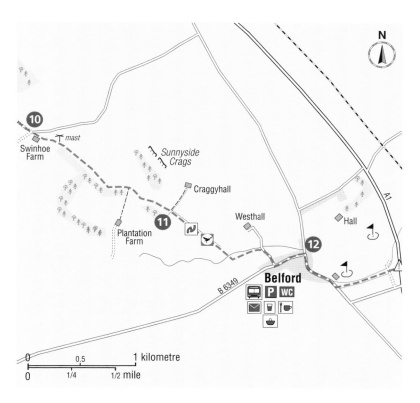

10
Swinhoe
Farm
mast

Sunnyside
Crags

Craggyhall

Plantation
Farm

11

Westhall

Hall

A1

12

B 6349

Belford

0   0.5   1 kilometre
0   1/4   1/2 mile

Belford

12 At the centre of the village, turn right along the former A1. Just after the entrance to the golf club, turn left on a path that runs alongside the Belford Burn. After crossing a track, follow the path to meet the present A1. Cross the road with care and go straight ahead on the footpath, past a large number of grain silos to reach the East Coast mainline railway.

Main East Coast Railway Line

St Oswald's Way crosses the East Coast main railway line from London (King's Cross) to Edinburgh three times. The Northumberland section of the railway began with the formation of the Newcastle and Berwick Company in 1845. Despite the opposition of Earl Grey, whose land it crossed, the line was opened two years later and provided a through route from York to Berwick – except for the later construction of bridges over the Tyne and the Tweed, which followed in 1849 and 1850.

13 Take great care when crossing the railway as high-speed trains frequently pass this point. Follow the path ahead into a field, then turn right through a gate and over a disused railway. Cross another field to reach a track. Go straight ahead then, at the next bend, go straight on across the field to a stile. Cross the stile and walk with the wall, then a hedge, on your right, looking eastwards towards Spindlestone Heughs.

Spindlestone Ducket

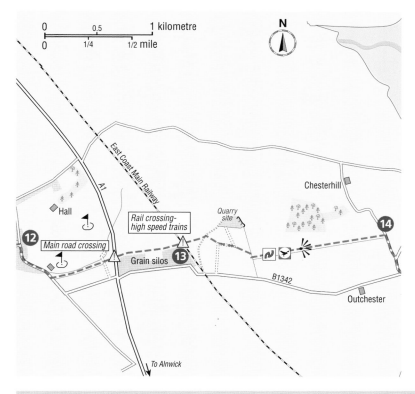

Spindlestone Ducket

The Ducket is a tall four-storey tower shown on maps as a windmill, although it is more likely to have been a dovecote. It dates from the 18th century and has a slate roof with a ball on top. The Ducket was built on the site of a medieval moated farmstead.

14 After reaching a lane, turn right. At the next junction, go straight on, and then turn left on a minor road to reach Spindlestone Ducket. Follow the road around to the left and down the hill. Just after crossing the Waren Burn at Spindlestone Mill, turn left and walk down the lane for 200 yards to a footpath. Turn right on the path, up through the wood, then along the left-hand edge of a field. Cross over a stile then walk along to another field.

Spindlestone Heughs

Spindlestone Heughs is one of a series of rocky outcrops of the Whin Sill in the Bamburgh area. It is a Site of Special Scientific Interest because of the unusual communities of plants that grow there.

On the Heughs there are also remains of an Iron Age fort or defended settlement. The natural cliffs were used as part of the defences, along with ditches and ramparts.

The Laidley Worm of Spindlestone Heughs is a ballad that was probably written in the 1770s. It tells the story of a king who brings home to Bamburgh a new wife who turns her stepdaughter into a 'Laidley Worm', a loathsome serpent or dragon. She is rescued by three kisses from her brother and they turn the queen's own spell back on her, changing her into a hideous toad.

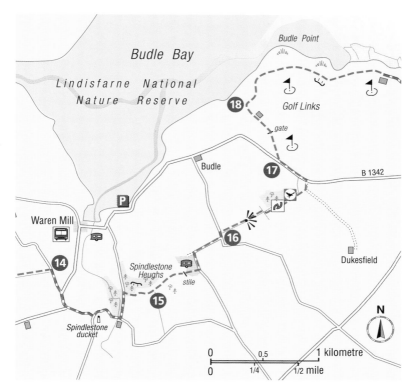

Budle Bay

Lindisfarne National Nature Reserve

Budle Point

18

Golf Links

gate

Budle

17

B 1342

P

Waren Mill

16

Dukesfield

14

Spindlestone Heughs

stile

15

Spindlestone ducket

N

0   0.5   1 kilometre

0   1/4   1/2 mile

15 Cross the corner of the field, then follow the path alongside a wall. To the left are the crags of Spindlestone Heughs. Carry straight on along the edge of a field, then go through a gate on the left, into a caravan site. Walk with the hedge on your right to reach a lane. Turn left and follow the lane to a T-junction.

16 Turn left, then right along a field-edge footpath with excellent views of Bamburgh and the coast. Follow the path ahead, through to a field with trees and crags on your left-hand side. Keep towards the top of the field, then go down to a stile and meet a lane. Turn left, then left again along the road verge.

17 At the top of the slope, turn right on a footpath across a golf course. Be aware of golf balls and follow the markers through the course. Lovely views across Budle Bay and towards Holy Island can be seen. Leave the course at a gate and head towards the Bay, around to the left of the buildings and along a track to a gate.

Budle Bay

Beautiful Budle Bay is part of the Lindisfarne National Nature Reserve and also features the site of the port of Warenmouth. The port was founded, as Bamburgh's port, in the mid 11th century. Warenmouth was able to accommodate boats of considerable size and was, at the time, England's most northerly port.

18 Follow the track to the right, then ahead through a gate and back onto the golf course. Follow the marked path down to the left until reaching a World War II pillbox. Turn right and follow the path through the dunes and overlooking the sea. At the golf clubhouse, follow the road towards Bamburgh.

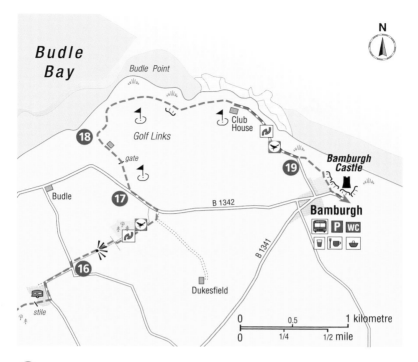

19 On reaching the houses, bear left on a track towards the castle, then left again on a footpath that leads you to the right of the castle. Follow the tarmac path around to the left of the cricket ground to the road. Go straight on towards the village, or turn sharp left along the road to the right of the castle.

Bamburgh Castle

Bamburgh

B 1340

St. Oswald's Way

0   1   2 kilometres
0   1/2   1 mile

N

Harbour

Seahouses

North
Sunderland

Beadnell

B 1340

Beadnell
Harbour

Beadnell Bay

High Newton
-by-the-Sea

Football Hole

B 1340

Low Newton
-by-the-Sea

Newton Haven

Embleton Bay

Embleton

Dunstanburgh
Castle

B 1339

Dunstan

Harbour

Craster

Distances from Bamburgh to:		
Seahouses		
4 miles	(6 km)	
Beadnell		
6½ miles	(10 km)	
Low Newton-by-the-Sea		
10 miles	(16 km)	
Craster		
14 miles	(22 km)	

Bamburgh

The imposing structure of Bamburgh Castle dominates this part of the Northumberland coast. Bamburgh was the site of King Oswald's royal headquarters but archaeology has revealed a long occupation of the site, probably dating back to an Iron Age hill fort.

The Anglo-Saxon Chronicle records that Bamburgh was founded by King Ida. He was (probably) Oswald's great grandfather and founder of the Bernician dynasty. However, there are no remains of Anglo-Saxon buildings at Bamburgh.

Bamburgh was an important royal stronghold until 1464 when, during the War of the Roses, it became the first English castle to be destroyed by gunfire. It was to remain a ruin until it was bought by Lord Crewe in the 18th century. In the 1890s, the castle was sold to the armament manufacturer Lord Armstrong who undertook the extensive re-building to convert the castle to a family country home, which it remains to this day.

There is a small archaeological museum within the castle that contains a number of interesting finds. From Oswald's era, these include fragments of a highly decorated stone chair (perhaps the

king's throne) and the remains of an extraordinarily sophisticated sword that could only have belonged to a king. A vast Anglo-Saxon cemetery of Oswald's time has been discovered to the south of the castle that, it is thought, may contain as many as 1,200 bodies.

Although the castle dominates the village, the rest of Bamburgh also has a fascinating history. In the 13th century it was home to a Dominican friary and also a leper colony! About that time, a group of Augustinian canons built the impressive

St. Aidan's Church

St. Aidan's Church. The church was heavily restored in the 19th century and contains a St. Oswald's Chapel.

At the church there is also a monument to Grace Darling, who was born in Bamburgh and famously rescued survivors of a shipwreck on the Farne Islands in 1838.

When tides allow, it is possible to walk from Bamburgh along the beach as far as the dunes to the north-west of Seahouses.

1 Leave Bamburgh on the main road out of the village, passing the castle. About 250 yards after the main village car park, bear right on a footpath across the field towards the right-hand buildings of those ahead (Redbarns). Pass just to the left of the buildings and follow the path ahead through the fields, often with the Cheviot Hills visible in the distance to your right and the Farne Islands out at sea to your left.

Farne Islands

There are 28 Farne Islands, although some are covered at high tide. The nearest of the larger islands is Inner Farne. This was the home, and favourite place, of St Cuthbert. He lived there from late in the 670s until 685 when he was persuaded to become Bishop of Lindisfarne.

Further out on the island of Longstone is a lighthouse. This was built in 1826 and its first keeper was William Darling, the father of Grace. The two of them carried out the famous rescue of survivors from the SS Forfarshire.

The Farnes are the home to thousands of breeding seabirds from late May until the end of July. Those numbering more than 1,000 pairs include arctic terns, sandwich terns, shags, kittiwakes, guillemots and puffins. Mention should also be made of St Cuthbert's own favourite eider ducks, known as Cuddy (or St Cuthbert) Ducks. There is also a large population of grey seals.

2 After passing Greenhill Farm to your left, walk with a wall on your left then over to a gate. Go through the gate and walk with a fence, then a hedge on your right. Turn right onto a track to

Eider (male)
© Uwe Ohse

reach Fowberry. Turn left along the lane and follow it through to a T-junction at Shoreston Hall. Turn right, then immediately left on a footpath. Follow the path ahead across two fields. In the third field, go straight on, then bear left around the corner of a field and towards the industrial units ahead.

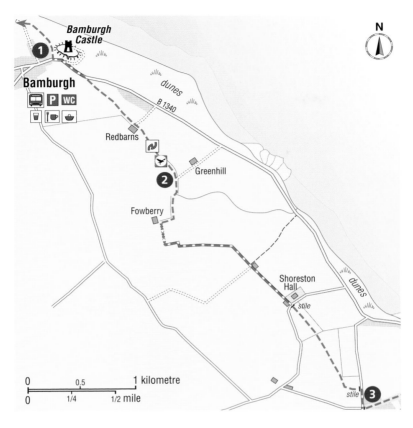

Bamburgh

- Bamburgh Castle
- dunes
- B 1340
- Redbarns
- Greenhill
- Fowberry
- Shoreston Hall
- stile
- dunes
- stile

0 | 0.5 | 1 kilometre
0 | 1/4 | 1/2 mile

N

3 At the road, turn right, then left on the cycle path opposite a junction. This path runs along the course of an old railway, skirting the village of North Sunderland before reaching the car park at Seahouses. Go straight on through the car park to reach the road.

Seahouses

Seahouses and North Sunderland

The path from North Sunderland follows the line of the former North Sunderland Light Railway. The railway was created in 1892 to provide a link between the main line at Chathill and North Sunderland and its port, Seahouses. The end of line is now the main car park.

Two rocky promontories have made Seahouses a natural harbour for at least 700 years. The development of the fishing trade in the 17th century, and lime burning in the early 18th century, led to the development of the harbour facilities. The limekilns that can be seen at the harbour continued in use until 1858.

On the rocks to the east of the harbour is a small stone building (the Powder House) that was built in 1886 to store gunpowder used to create the Long Pier and New Harbour.

Today, Seahouses is a major tourist centre and the port for boat trips to the Farne Islands.

4 Turn left, then right, down to the harbour. Follow the road around to the right of the harbour, then walk on a footpath along the coast. The path then enters a golf course – be aware of flying golf balls as you follow the waymark posts through the course. Go straight ahead for 50 yards then turn right along a path to reach a gateway. Follow the driveway ahead to a road. Turn left and walk along the roadside path with Annstead Dunes Nature Reserve to your left.

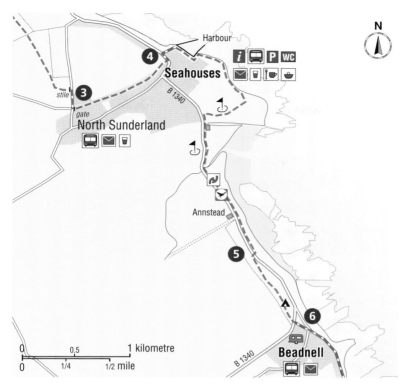

5 300 yards after Annstead Farm, take the path into the field on your right as the road bends to the left. (The route may be diverted in future years as the roadside path is extended to Beadnell.) Walk with the stone wall over to your right and cross into the next field at a stile. Walk alongside the stone wall, then through to the far end of a campsite. Turn right, then left towards Beadnell village.

6 Follow the road towards the harbour for half a mile. At the junction, it is possible to bear left for an interesting visit to Beadnell Harbour and, perhaps, an alternative route along the beach of Beadnell Bay. St. Oswald's Way, however, follows the road around to the right and past the car park.

Beadnell

The attractive village of Beadnell includes the interesting parish church of St. Ebba, who was the sister of St. Oswald. One of the village pubs, the Craster Arms, contains the remains of a medieval tower house.

On the rocks to the north-east of Beadnell Harbour (known as Ebb's Nook) are the remains of the medieval chapel of St. Ebba. It was excavated in 1853 and the remains suggested that it had been built not long after Aidan's arrival at Lindisfarne. Little is known of the chapel although the name suggests a link with Oswald's sister.

The impressive group of three large, and disused, limekilns that stand near the harbour were built in 1798 and are now in the care of the National Trust. Limekilns were used to produce lime by burning limestone with coal. The lime was widely used to improve the quality of agricultural land.

The harbour is of a similar date to the kilns and has the distinction of being the only west-facing harbour on the east coast of England.

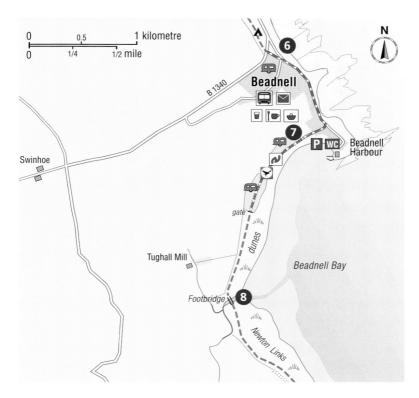

Long Nanny Burn

7 Take the left-hand option of the two driveways and walk with the caravan park on your right and the dunes on your left. Then enter a second caravan park and follow the driveway. After 200 yards, take the right-hand fork and follow this through to a gate into rough land on the edge of the dunes. Follow the path ahead past Tughall Dunes and through to a footbridge over the Long Nanny Burn.

8 Continue straight on along the main path through Newton Links. After passing Newton Links House and through a gate, you arrive at a car park.

Newton Links

Newton Links is one of the best examples of sand dunes with species-rich vegetation on the Northumberland Coast, and has been designated as a Site of Special Scientific Interest (SSSI). The site also includes saltmarsh around the Long Nanny inlet and a colony of little terns.

9 Walk up the road away from the car park, then turn left through a gateway after a few yards. Go towards the path that runs along the back of the dunes and follow it, eventually bearing right to reach some small crags. Follow the path to the right of the crags, then along the edge of a field, with Dunstanburgh Castle in the distance. Pass through a gateway then head across the field to the small village of Low Newton-by-the-Sea and turn left at the road.

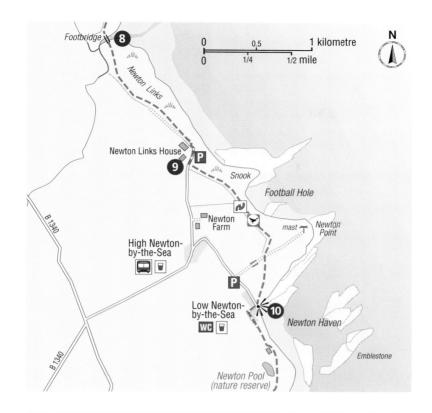

Low Newton-by-the-Sea

The Square at Low Newton with buildings around three sides and the sea along the fourth are 18th century fisherman's cottages. The only two-storey building in The Square is the pub, The Ship Inn. The cottages were improved in the middle of the 19th century. This was necessary, apparently, as a contemporary writer described them as "not pretty nor pleasing". This is not a description that applies today as they are excellently preserved.

The building on the hilltop to the north of The Square is a coastguard station. It was built in the early 19th century and provides a splendid view down the coast to Dunstanburgh Castle.

10 It is possible to walk along the beach at Embleton Bay as an alternative route, when tides allow. Otherwise, turn right just before The Square at the bottom of the village. Follow the access road around the back of the cottages and pub. Go straight ahead on a track parallel to the coast. Pass to the left of a cottage on a footpath into Newton Pool Nature Reserve. Follow the paths around to the right and up to the top of a slope, overlooking the Pool.

Newton Pool

Newton Pool

Just to the south of Low Newton is Newton Pool Nature Reserve, owned by the National Trust. The reserve is set behind the dunes and is a freshwater pool ringed with rushes and with a number of islands. There are hides from which migrant waders and wildfowl can often be seen, especially in winter.

Embleton Bay

11 Turn left and follow the path to the left of the golf course and past the beach huts, with wonderful views across Embleton Bay. The path then drops down a bank and runs through rough ground to the left of the golf course. After reaching a stream and bridge on your left, turn right onto the path across the course.

12 Just before reaching the club house car park, turn left and follow the path around and along the edge of the golf course.

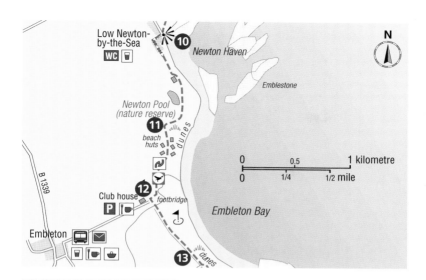

Whin Sill

The frequently dramatic features of the Great Whin Sill are seen at a number of places along the path. One of the most spectacular outcrops is at Bamburgh Castle. Others are along much of Hadrian's Wall and, out at sea, the Farne Islands. Lindisfarne Castle and Dunstanburgh Castle are also built on the Whin Sill.

The Whin Sill is composed of the medium-grained hard rock known as dolomite and was formed by molten rock forced through layers of earlier rock by the movement of the earth's tectonic plates. The name derives from terms used by northern English quarrymen. 'Sill' was used to describe a more or less horizontal body of rock and 'whin' was used to describe dark and hard rocks.

Dunstanburgh Castle

The second Earl of Lancaster, grandson of King Henry III, had the original castle built in 1313-6. Lancaster was the leading – and richest - noble in England and had stormy relations with the then king, Edward II (as he did with nearly everybody else). Dunstanburgh was conceived as a safe retreat and he wanted, and got, an immense and lavishly equipped castle. He was never to use it for its purpose: when he led a rebellion against the king in 1322, he was captured at Boroughbridge in Yorkshire and subsequently beheaded before he could retreat to Dunstanburgh.

In the early 15th century, the castle fell into some disrepair and it was not until the late 1430s that major repairs were carried out. Later that century, during the Wars of the Roses, Dunstanburgh was successfully attacked three times and much damage was done.

The remains that are seen today date mainly from the earliest period. The huge scale of the castle can be appreciated from the surviving walls enclosing 11 acres and the grandeur from what is left of the gatehouse. This gatehouse, with the inner ward behind, was the main domestic quarters of the castle. Further along the south wall is the Constable's Tower, which was the residence of the castle's commanding officer, and, at the end of the wall, Egyncleugh Tower. The other remaining tower, Lilburn Tower, is in the west wall and was probably a watchtower.

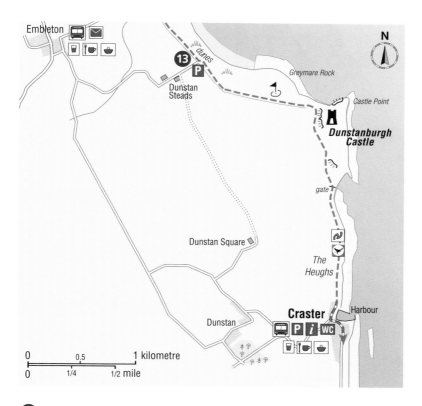

13 Pass the parking area near Dunstan Steads and follow the main path to the right of the golf course. Finally cross the course and head towards the dramatic cliffs of Rumble Churn and Castle Point. Pass to the right of Dunstanburgh Castle along the path at the bottom of the slope. Follow the path southwards to reach a gate. Join the main path and continue on to the village of Craster.

Craster Harbour

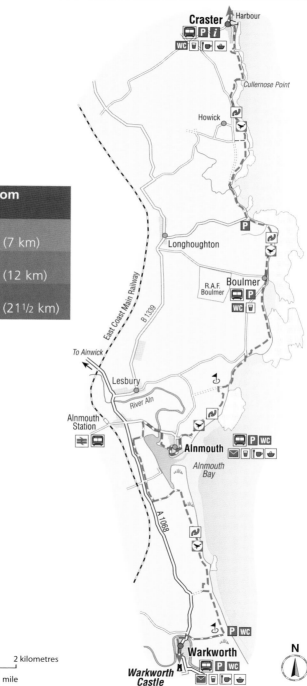

Distances from Craster to:

Boulmer
4½ miles   (7 km)

Alnmouth
7½ miles   (12 km)

Warkworth
13½ miles   (21½ km)

St. Oswald's Way

0   1   2 kilometres

0   1/2   1 mile

Craster

The village of Craster is grouped around the distinctive small harbour. The harbour only took its present shape in the late 1930s when the silos that had stood above the (remaining) arch at the end of the south pier were removed. These silos had been constructed in 1914 to assist in the shipping of whinstone. The quarry at Craster provided stone that was used for kerbs in London and Roker Pier in Sunderland. The quarry is now partly a car park and also the Northumberland Wildlife Trust's Arnold Memorial Reserve.

Craster has another claim to fame - kippers. Herring fishing has been a long established occupation and the first smokehouse, dating from 1856, remains operating to this day. Robson's still make Craster Kippers even though the herring no longer comes from the North Sea. To the west of the harbour is Craster Tower, which originated as a fortified pele tower. Originally the village clustered around the tower and only developed around the harbour in around 1700. Craster offers dramatic views of Dunstanburgh Castle to the north – a view that was painted by JMW Turner.

1 From the centre of Craster, walk along the road to the right of the harbour. Turn left just before the Jolly Fisherman pub, then right through the gate at the back of the building. Follow the path past the village and along the coast. Pass the spectacular cliffs of Cullernose Point and continue along the coastal path to The Bathing House.

The Geology of the Northumberland Coast

The Northumberland coastline is made of a variety of types of rock, which play a major role in the landscape, wildlife and human activity of the area. This section of the walk shows some of the more interesting geology that can be found.

From Craster southwards to the cliffs of Cullernose Point, the coastal rocks are made of whinstone, part of the Whin Sill, as described in Section 2. The cliffs provide a safe nesting spot for fulmars and other seabirds.

The next mile or two of the path runs along sedimentary rocks including limestone and sandstone. These rocks are more easily eroded and small, sandy bays have formed in a number of places. The bay at Rumbling Kern is surrounded by cliffs of sandstone that has been quarried in the past.

Either side of Boulmer, the rock changes again to a type of coarse-grained sandstone, known here as the Longhoughton Grit. The outcrops of this rock extend out to sea, forming reefs or 'steels'. A geological fault at Boulmer has resulted in a gap in the reef and allowed the development of a safe harbour.

Rumbling Kern

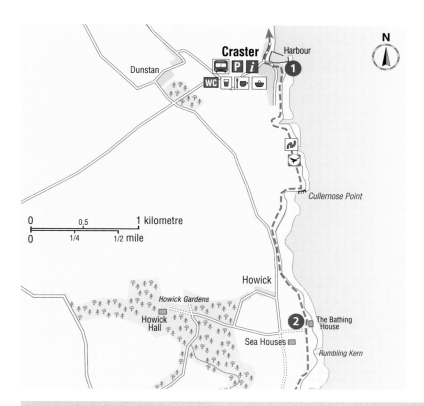

Dunstan

Craster

Harbour

N

Cullernose Point

0 0.5 1 kilometre
0 1/4 1/2 mile

Howick

Howick Gardens

Howick Hall

Sea Houses

The Bathing House

Rumbling Kern

The Bathing House

The Bathing House is a (private) 18th century cottage that was remodelled in the 1840s for the Grey Family. Steps led from the cottage to a quarried out rock pool. Further inland is the Grey's Howick Hall. Among the owners of Howick Hall was the second Earl Grey who was the prime minister responsible for the Great Reform Act of 1832. He also gave his name to Earl Grey tea. The gardens at Howick are regularly open to the public.

2 After passing the building, bear left on the path southwards along the coast. Three-quarters of a mile further on, you pass the site of Howick's Stone Age settlement to your right. Follow the track ahead and along past the small parking area at Low Stead Links.

Howick Stone Age Settlement

Excavations by archaeologists in 2000 to 2002 at Howick Haven revealed the remains of a mesolithic hut dating from just after 8,000 BC – possibly the oldest house yet found in Britain. The people living in this Stone Age hut were 'hunter-gatherers' since they would have obtained their food by hunting, gathering and fishing. At that time, the sea was about four and a half metres below today's level. The hut was similar to a tepee and a hut based upon this discovery has been constructed at the Maelmin Heritage Trail, at Milfield near Wooler. A smaller version now stands at Howick.

3 Continue along the track towards Boulmer and cross a footbridge. Follow the track, then the road into the village of Boulmer.

Boulmer

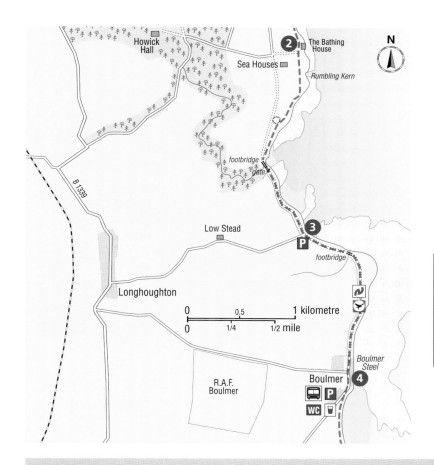

Boulmer

Boulmer was known as the smuggling capital of Northumberland in the 18th and early 19th centuries. The smugglers came to Boulmer from much of Northumberland and the Scottish Borders for gin brought from Holland. The names of a number of the smugglers are recorded: among them Wull Balmer of Jedburgh, Jock Melvin, Wull Faa of Kirk Yetholm and Isaac Addison, one time landlord of Boulmer's inn, the Fishing Boat.

Today, Boulmer is better known for its RAF station. RAF Boulmer began in 1940 as a decoy airfield to attract enemy planes away from the real airfield at Acklington, a few miles to the south. Amongst its various roles now, it is the headquarters of No 202 Squadron. This squadron operates the yellow Sea King helicopters that provide search and rescue services in northern England and southern Scotland.

4 Go straight ahead at the junction in the village then, after the right-hand bend, turn left onto a footpath that runs along the coast. Walk through the car parking area, then along a track and through a gate. Follow the path ahead past the large navigation posts and on to reach a caravan park.

Boulmer

5 Turn right on a grassy track past the caravans and towards Seaton House. Follow the track past Seaton House then turn left on a track opposite the last building. Bear right on a footpath and walk alongside a fence past the wooden huts to reach a track onto the beach.

6 Walk along the beach to the right. Just before the buildings on the right, leave the beach through a gate and follow the path uphill. Pass to the right of the golf clubhouse, then turn left on a footpath onto the golf course. Turn left again across the course towards the sea. Follow the path along the coast and back onto the golf course.

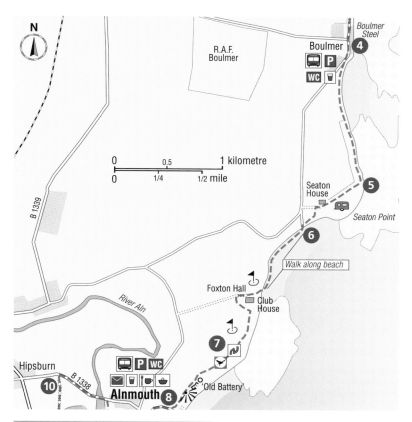

The Old Battery

7 Walk alongside the fence through the course and be aware of flying golf balls. Follow the path ahead through the rough ground. At the Old Battery on the left, bear left on the path down to the road on the edge of another golf course.

Old Battery and Coastal Defences

The Old Battery, a gun emplacement, was built in 1881 by the Duke of Northumberland for the use of the Percy Artillery Volunteers. It has a small, rectangular room and an ammunition store below ground level.

It is similar to the more recent pillboxes - small, squat concrete forts with slits for guns - that can be seen at many points along the coast. The threat of German invasion from across the North Sea during the Second World War led to the construction of coastal defences along the East and South coasts. These were hurriedly built in 1940. In Northumberland the defences consist mainly of pillboxes and concrete blocks. The concrete blocks, which are usually cubes about a metre high, will be found along long stretches of beach. Their purpose was to impede the movement of tanks.

8 Turn right along the tarmac path parallel to the road as far as a junction. Turn left along the road, around to the bottom of the main street through Alnmouth.

Church Hill from Alnmouth

Alnmouth

Alnmouth, or St. Waleric as it was originally called, was founded as a medieval borough in the 12th century. It was to develop as a grain port and shipbuilding centre until 1336, when the village was virtually destroyed by the Scots. Twelve years later, the Black Death wiped out one third of the population.

In the 17th and 18th centuries, the port thrived again by exporting grain from the Tyne valley and, at one time, there were 16 granaries in the village. Smuggling was also a large part of Alnmouth life and it was described as "a small seaport town famous for its wickedness" by John Wesley, the founder of the Methodist Church.

In those days, a narrow ridge of land linked Alnmouth with Church Hill, which can be seen across the mouth of the river. The River Aln entered the sea to the south of Church Hill until 1806, when a violent storm breached the ridge and changed the course of the river. This made the harbour much less attractive for shipping, as the new channel was less deep than the old one.

The growth of tourism in Victorian times helped Alnmouth to recover, leading to the picturesque, peaceful village of today.

9 Bear left onto Riverside Road and follow it around the Aln Estuary. Just after a recreation area, turn left on a footpath known as Lovers Walk. Follow the path around to meet the road at The Duchess's Bridge. Cross the road then turn left over the footbridge alongside the road bridge. Walk along the road for 600 yards, then turn left onto a track between fields (part of the Coast and Castles Cycle Route).

Alnmouth

10 Follow the cycle track between the fields then parallel to the road. At the second junction, turn left and head along the track towards the sea and past the estuary. Follow the track around to the right, with the dunes on your left and the old guano shed on the right.

Coast and Castles Cycle Route

This popular cycling trail runs from Newcastle to Edinburgh, a distance of 200 miles, including much of the Northumberland coast. It is also part of an even longer route, the National Cycle Network Route 1, which runs all the way from Dover to John O' Groats.

11 As an alternative, when the tide allows, you can make your way through the dunes to the beach, then along towards Warkworth Dunes. St. Oswald's Way continues along the track, through a gate, then straight ahead on the path parallel to the coastline. Follow the path up onto and along the dunes.

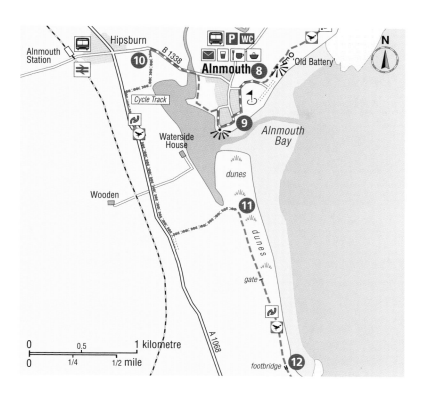

Aln Estuary

The estuary of the River Aln contains the largest area of mature saltmarsh between Lindisfarne and the Tees Estuary. Saltmarsh is a habitat that forms where boggy ground is flooded by seawater when the tide is high. It provides a home for rare plants and a good source of food for waders and other birds. Many of the country's saltmarshes have been converted into farmland.

The saltmarsh is part of the Alnmouth Saltmarsh and Dunes Site of Special Scientific Interest (SSSI), which features several plant species that are at or near the northern limit of their range in Britain. Further to the south lies another important site for nature conservation, the Warkworth Dunes and Saltmarsh SSSI. The dunes there support an exceptional range of plants and invertebrates.

The building near to the track by the Aln Estuary is said to be an old guano storage shed. Alnmouth used to import guano (bird droppings used as fertiliser), and this spot would have been far enough away from the village to keep the dreadful smell at bay.

⑫ After crossing a footbridge, bear right on a track through a caravan park then along the edge of a golf course, with lovely views ahead to Coquet Island and Amble. Watch out for flying golf balls as the track crosses the course. Follow the track along the other side of the course then, after a gate, turn left on a path. Cross the golf course again and walk under a long bridge until almost reaching the beach.

Coquet Island

Coquet Island is about a mile off the coast and it and its white square lighthouse are clearly visible from the path. The lighthouse was built in 1841 and its first lighthouse keeper was Grace Darling's brother.

The island has many religious connections and was famous for its monastery in Anglo-Saxon times. Later, there was a hermitage on the island: Henry, the hermit of Coquet Island, is buried at Tynemouth.

Today, the island is managed by the Royal Society for the Protection of Birds. It has a large number of puffins and is particularly famous for a small colony of roseate terns. Landing is not allowed on the island but boat trips around it are available in late spring and summer from Amble.

Puffins
© Thomas O'Neil

⑬ Turn right along the path through the dunes. Follow the path ahead, with the dunes on your left and the golf course on your right, to reach a track.

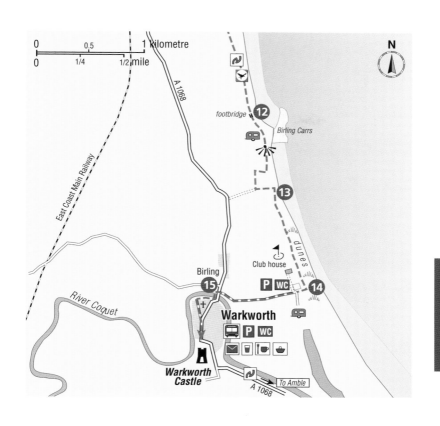

0   0.5   1 kilometre
0   1/4   1/2 mile

N

A 1068

East Coast Main Railway

footbridge

12

Birling Carrs

13

dunes

Club house

Birling

15

P   WC   **14**

River Coquet

Warkworth

**Warkworth
Castle**

To Amble

A 1068

Warkworth Dunes

14 Turn right and follow the track ahead up to Warkworth Dunes Picnic Site. Carry straight on along the road and down to a junction on the edge of Warkworth.

15 Cross the road carefully and cross the River Coquet on the old bridge. Go through the gatehouse then turn sharp right onto a riverside path. Follow this path (Monks Walk) until you reach a parking area. Turn left past St. Lawrence's Church and into the centre of the village.

Monks Walk

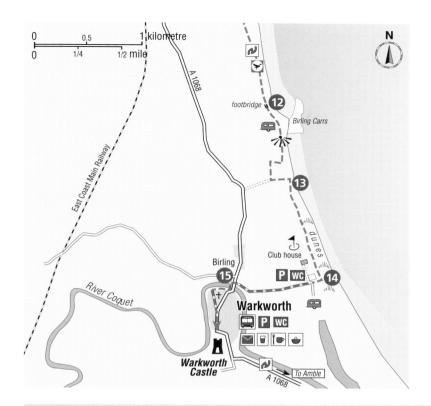

Warkworth Bridge and Gatehouse

The older bridge over the Coquet at Warkworth was built in the last quarter of the 14th century. It has two arches and a gatehouse at the south end. The road into the village used to run through the archway at the gatehouse, which guarded the entrance to the bridge. Warkworth Bridge is one of only two fortified medieval bridges in Britain – the other is in Monmouth.

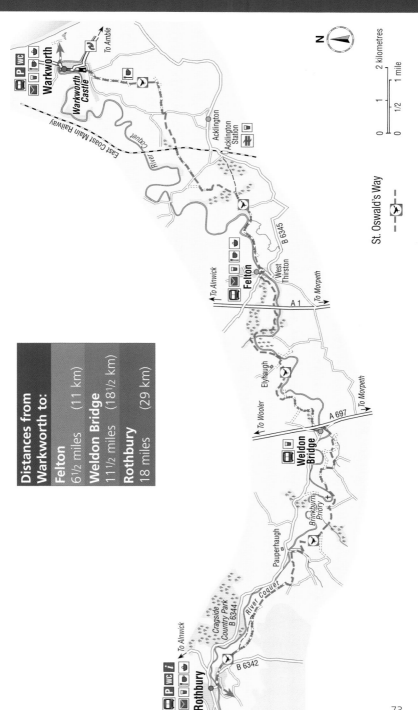

Warkworth

Warkworth Castle

To Amble

East Coast Main Railway

River Coquet

Acklington
Acklington Station

N

0   1   2 kilometres
0   1/2   1 mile

St. Oswald's Way

B 6345

Felton
West Thirston

To Alnwick

To Morpeth

A 1

Elyhaugh

To Wooler

To Morpeth

A 697

Weldon Bridge

Brinkburn Priory

Pauperhaugh

Cragside Country Park

River Coquet

B 6344

To Alnwick

B 6342

Rothbury

Distances from Warkworth to:

Felton
6½ miles   (11 km)

Weldon Bridge
11½ miles   (18½ km)

Rothbury
18 miles   (29 km)

Warkworth

The old village of Warkworth is enclosed in a loop of the River Coquet and is of Anglo-Saxon origin. There was a Saxon church here founded by King Ceolwulf in the 730s and the present early 12th century church of St. Lawrence stands on its site. Much of this Norman church remains today, although there have been later additions. The village also has a number of fine buildings of the 18th and 19th centuries and most of Castle Street is of this date.

The village, however, is dominated by the castle – "this worm-eaten hold of ragged stone", according to Shakespeare's induction to Henry IV Part 2. Nevertheless, the castle was substantially finished by Shakespeare's time.

The earliest castle was an 11th century 'motte and bailey'. In 1158, Henry II gave Warkworth to Roger FitzRichard who began the building of the first stone castle and of this period the gatehouse survives. Ownership eventually passed to Henry de Percy IV, who became the first Earl of Northumberland, and had the keep built in the 1380s and 90s. Today, the keep is the most intact building at the castle.

The ownership of Warkworth Castle passed back and forth between the Percy family and the royal family for centuries. Eventually, the cost of maintaining the castle was so great that the Percys gave it to the nation in 1922. It is now cared for by English Heritage.

Reached by boat from the south of the Coquet is the unusual 14th century structure of Warkworth Hermitage. The chapel and the adjoining sanctuary were carved out of the sandstone rock in about 1330-40. They are fairly small (the chapel itself is just over six metres by two metres) and a great deal of skill must have been needed to carve out the architectural detail. In the 15th century, small domestic buildings were added to the face of the rock.

According to tradition, the first hermit and builder of the hermitage was Sir Bertram, a knight who mistakenly killed his lover, Lady Isabel Widdrington, and his brother as he tried to rescue her from the Scots, causing him to renounce the world.

1 From the centre of Warkworth, head up the street towards the castle. Instead of turning left with the road at the top, go straight ahead on a footpath that runs to the right of the castle. Ignore the path that goes down to the river and go straight on, passing the castle. Follow the surfaced path past the clubhouse and ground of Warkworth Cricket Club to reach a road.

2 Turn right, then left onto Guilden Road, and right again along Warkworth Avenue. At the end of the road, bear left on the track to New Barns. Carry straight on past the farm buildings at New Barns. Follow the track ahead then between the fields. At a junction (2/3 mile after New Barns), turn right and follow the old track, with the water tower on your right, until reaching a road.

New Barns and Morwick

To the south of New Barns is an area that was part of the large Chester House opencast coal workings. The area was restored to farmland, with tracks and hedges, in 1999. The funnel-like structure on the hill nearby is a concrete water tower that was constructed in 1970.

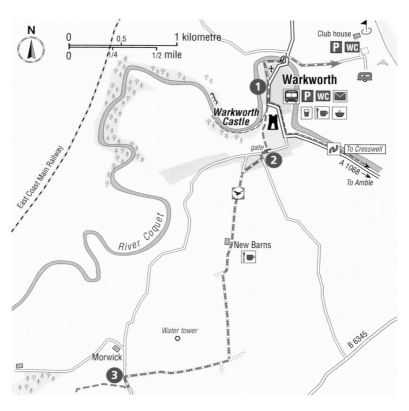

Opencast restoration

3 Cross the road when safe and turn left. Walk along the side of the road for 100 yards, then turn right along a bridleway (Rake Lane). Follow the winding, grassy old lane and, when reaching the bridge, go straight ahead under the railway. Continue along the lane until reaching a road.

4 Go straight ahead on the bridleway opposite, until reaching a stone track. Carry straight on and follow the track, passing a pond on your left, and into a field. Turn right and follow the path, with the field boundary on your right. Join a track and go straight ahead to the corner of the field.

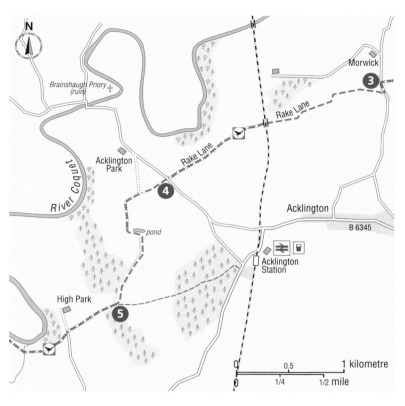

5 Turn right through the gateway and follow the track to a lane. Turn left, then immediately right on a public footpath. Follow the path to the Coquet and walk along the riverside through to the road at West Thirston. Cross the road then cross the River Coquet into Felton using the Old Bridge.

Felton

The village of Felton lay on the old Great North Road and the village developed as a staging post with inns, shops and services. The Old Bridge across the Coquet was built in the 15th century but is now for pedestrians only.

A key date in Felton's history was 1216. The Northern barons, unwilling to pay taxes to the English King John, had met at Felton Park in the previous year and decided to do homage to the Scottish King Alexander – John had the village burnt down. Some 500 years later, Felton Park was to be a base for the Jacobite rebellion of 1715. The village took a different view in 1745 and welcomed the Duke of Cumberland who passed through on his way to fight at Culloden against the Jacobites. He is said to have referred to Felton as a "loyal little village".

Felton's large and interesting Church of St. Michael and All Angels has a high 19th century roof over its chancel and very low roofs elsewhere. Much of the rest of the church dates from the 13th and 14th centuries with the belfry having been rebuilt some 300 years later.

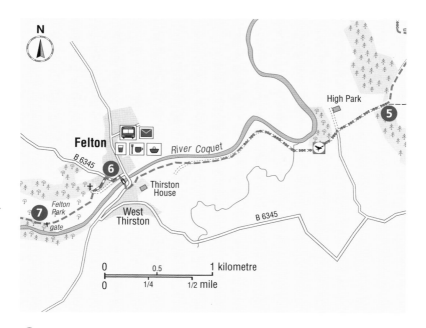

6 Turn left after the bridge, then follow the road to the right at the war memorial. At the next junction, turn left towards the Church of St. Michael and All Angels. At the church that, contrary to first impressions, really does have a roof, bear left on a track then through a gate into a field. Follow the track, then bear slightly left on the footpath across the field.

7 Pass through a gate into the edge of some woodland. Follow the path along the top of the bank, with the river down to the left through the trees. Pass under the A1 then up a flight of steps to a gate. Bear left on a woodland track and follow it ahead for 3/4 mile. Bear left off the track, following the waymarked public footpath to the riverbank and along to a footbridge.

8 Turn left after the bridge and walk uphill. Bear left at the path junction before the top of the slope. Follow the path through the fields, parallel to the river, to reach a gate in top corner of a field. After the gate, follow the path gradually down to the bottom edge of the field with the fence and the Coquet to your left, to reach the far corner.

River Coquet and Coquet Valley Woodlands SSSI

The River Coquet flows for about 57 miles (90km) across Northumberland, from the Cheviot Hills to the sea below Warkworth. It is a relatively natural fast-flowing upland river with characteristic wildlife. The Coquet is one of the most important angling rivers in the north of England, with large runs of sea trout and salmon.

The lower and middle reaches of the river provide undisturbed habitat for otters, and the rich insect life also provides food for a wide variety of bat colonies that roost and rear their young within the valley, particularly around Brinkburn Priory.

The Coquet valley has several woodlands that are long-established and relatively unmodified by planting. There are few such woodlands now left in Northumberland and most are confined to steep river valleys, as along the Coquet below Rothbury.

These excellent wildlife habitats have led to the river, and much of the land adjacent to it, being designated as a Site of Special Scientific Interest.

Otter
© Lynsey Allan

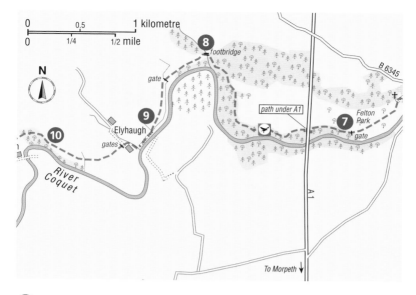

9 Cross the stile in the corner of the field and walk through to a track along the riverbank. Follow the track away from the river, then turn left up the hill and around to the right of the cottage. Go through the gate and cross the parking area to another small gate. Bear right across the field to a stile.

Follow the path ahead with the field boundary on your left as far as a gateway. Cross the field on the path to another gate.

10 Follow the path around the edge of this field then into some woodland on the left. Head through the trees then follow the path through grassland down to a gate near a house (Catheugh) on the left. Follow the track up through the field and towards High Weldon. Leave the track as it turns right and head along the path between the buildings. Follow the path straight on and eventually through to Low Weldon.

11 Pass the buildings and follow the driveway as it bends around to the right. Go straight ahead until you meet a road. Turn right and walk along the verge on the outside bend, under the bridge and on to the second junction on the left. Cross the road carefully then head down the side-road into Weldon Bridge.

Weldon Bridge

Weldon Bridge has an unusual design, with three elliptical arches and circular openings in-between. It was built in the 18th century and replaced two earlier ones – built in 1744 and 1752 – that had been swept away by floods. The Anglers Arms was a coaching inn on the old turnpike road from Morpeth to Cornhill-on-Tweed. It is an 18th century building with a large south-west wing added in the early part of the 19th century.

12 Walk past the Anglers Arms and bear left, crossing the bridge over the River Coquet. After 100 yards, turn right on a footpath through a

Weldon Bridge

riverside woodland. After crossing a footbridge, follow the field edge around to the left until reaching a gate. Bear right, across the corner of the field, to another gate.

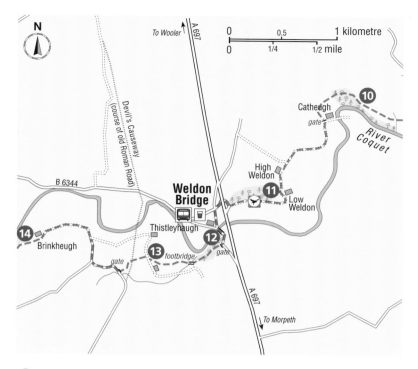

13 Cross the track, then walk up the left-hand side of the field until a stile on the left. Bear left over the stile, then walk around to the right, between the bushes and down to a lane. Turn right along the lane, then bear right again at the first junction. Go straight ahead along the lane, then turn left along a stone track to reach farm buildings (Brinkheugh).

Brinkheugh

The Devil's Causeway

The Devil's Causeway is the route of the major Roman road that runs south-west across Northumberland, from the mouth of the River Tweed at Berwick to meet Dere Street (the Roman York to Edinburgh road) just to the north of Portgate on Hadrian's Wall. It is possible that Oswald and his army followed the Devil's Causeway southwards to reach Heavenfield.

14 Keep to the left of the sheds and barns then pass the farmhouse to reach a gate. Follow the waymarked path ahead, keeping to the right-hand side of fields. Through the woodland to your right, you can catch glimpses of

Middleheugh

Brinkburn Priory across the river. Follow the path around to the right and continue to walk with the woodland on your right-hand side, eventually reaching the farm of Middleheugh.

Brinkburn Priory

A loop in the river provides the setting for Brinkburn Priory on the opposite bank. The priory was founded around 1135 by William Bertram I, Baron of Mitford for Augustinian canons – these were ordained monks and, since they wore a black habit, were known as Black Canons. They did not lead a solitary life but also had pastoral duties. For example, during the priory's existence, the vicar of Felton was a canon of Brinkburn. All that survives today of the priory is the church, a fine late Norman building dating from 1190 -1220 that was carefully restored in 1858.

The other main building on the site is the Manor House. After the dissolution of the monasteries, some of the buildings, probably little altered, were used as a house by George Fenwick. Although there are some 13th century remains in the basement, the building standing today was built in 1810 and extensively extended to the west in 1830-7. Last inhabited in 1952, the building was almost destroyed by extensive dry rot. Only the ground floor and some of the basement can be visited. Both buildings are in the care of English Heritage.

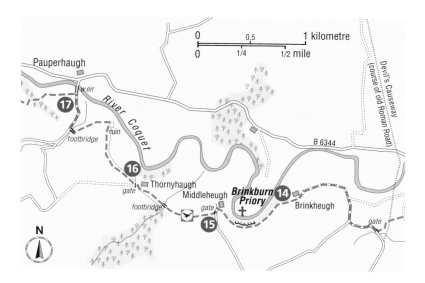

15 Cross the track near the entrance to the farmstead and follow the footpath. After a small gate, bear slightly left across the next field to a gate and stile. Go over the stile, cross the field towards the corner of a wood then go down the bank to a footbridge. Head up the opposite bank and bear left towards the far corner of the field. Cross the stile and pass to the left of Thornyhaugh farmhouse and buildings, then head along the track towards a gate.

16 Go through the gate then bear right across towards the right-hand side of the field. Follow the path through the fields, with excellent views of the Coquet valley and of the Simonside Hills to your left. The path leads eventually down to a stile by the ruin of Longhaugh. Turn left after the stile and walk along the edge of the field. Follow the path ahead through the next field to a gate and footbridge on your right. Cross the footbridge then turn right along the road until just before Pauperhaugh Bridge.

17 Turn left on a footpath and cross the field towards the far right-hand corner. Walk along the riverside path through the next field then turn left to reach the woodland. Go through the gate and head up the path through the trees. Enter a field then bear left around the top of a bank to meet a fence. Turn right and walk with the fence on your left until reaching an old cottage. Turn right and follow the main path to a gate. After the gate, turn right onto a lane.

18 Go through the gateway towards West Raw. Follow the track to the left of the buildings then around to the left and ahead through the fields. The track turns into a path and eventually passes the old cottage of Craghead. In the next field, bear left towards a gate and stile.

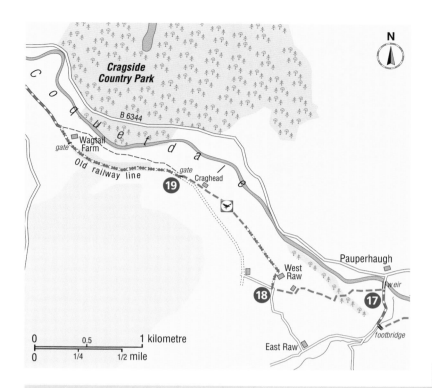

N

Cragside Country Park

B 6344

gate Wagtail Farm

Old railway line gate Craghead

19

West Raw

Pauperhaugh

weir

18

17

East Raw

footbridge

| 0 | 0.5 | 1 kilometre |
| 0 | 1/4 | 1/2 mile |

The Northumberland Central Railway

The former railway is the Northumberland Central Railway from Scots Gap to Rothbury. It was opened in 1870 and was originally conceived as an alternative route to Scotland. However, it was only a single track and never went further than Rothbury. It linked to the Wansbeck Valley Railway at Scots Gap. Both companies were to become part of the North British Railway. Passenger services ceased in September 1952 and the last goods train ran on the line in 1963.

19 Cross onto a disused railway line and head along it to your right. Pass Wagtail Farm on your right then, after passing the remains of an old bridge, bear left along a lane. From this lane, on the other side of the valley, the Cragside Estate can be seen. Follow the lane until meeting a road, then head down the hill into Rothbury. St. Oswald's Way does not go into the centre of the village, which can be reached by crossing one of the bridges over the river.

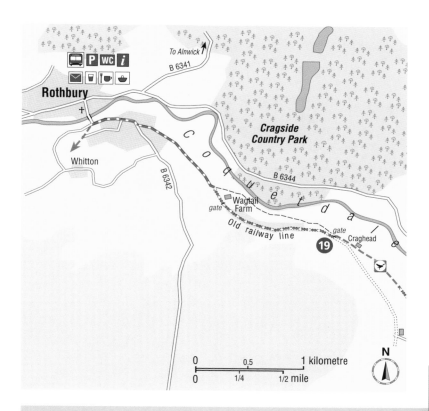

Cragside

Lord Armstrong, the armaments manufacturer, came to Cragside in 1863 and had a house built there as a country retreat. From 1869, that house was vastly extended and changed into a dramatic Victorian mansion. It was the first house in the world to be lit by electricity, derived from water power in the grounds.

The grounds were eventually extended to 1,700 acres and were transformed from a hillside into an amazing pleasure garden with

a six-miles long carriage drive and some 40 miles of paths. It has been suggested that seven million shrubs and trees were planted on the estate. Huge amounts of earth and rocks were moved to create rock gardens, lakes and streams. Cragside is now owned by the National Trust.

Cragside
© Gail Johnson

To Elsdon

Rothbury

B 6341

River Coquet

Whitton

Lordenshaws

B 6342

Simonside Hills
429m

NORTHUMBERLAND

NATIONAL

PARK

Coquet Cairn

Harwood
Forest

Fallowlees

Harwood
Forest

Harwood

**Distances from
Rothbury to:**

Lordenshaws car park
2½ miles (3½ km)

Harwood
9½ miles (15 km)

Knowesgate
13½ miles (22 km)

Kirkwhelpington
15 miles (24 km)

B 6342

To Otterburn

Catcherside

A 696

Knowesgate

Kirkwhelpington

To Newcastle

St. Oswald's Way

- - -◆- - -

0   1   2 kilometres

0   1/2   1 mile

N

Rothbury

The earliest settlers in the Rothbury area left their mark locally both in the 'cup and ring' markings on stones at Lordenshaws and in many neolithic graves, especially on the Simonside Hills. The later Celtic inhabitants dwelt mainly in the hill forts that were built on many local summits. Although defeated by the Romans, they were never really assimilated and remained faithful to their former way of life.

Rothbury was probably founded early in the Anglo-Saxon era – that is some time after 547, when King Ida first invaded Northumberland and set up his capital at Bamburgh. The name

Rothbury is thought to derive from a local Anglo-Saxon chieftain's personal name, meaning 'Hrotha's town'. It is suggested that Hrotha controlled quite a large slice of territory, with Rothbury at its centre, as there are two other places, Rothley and Rothhill, in the area.

The earliest relic of the old town is the remains of a fine old Anglo-Saxon cross dating back to about 800, part of which can still be seen in the All Saints Church – the remainder is now in

the Museum of Antiquities, in Newcastle. The church stands on the site of a much earlier Anglo-Saxon building but was rebuilt in the 13th century and extensively altered in 1850, though some 13th century work can still be seen.

Rothbury gradually became an important local market town, gaining its Charter in 1291. It suffered greatly, however, during the wars between England and Scotland and a castle was built on Haw Hill, close to the church. Unfortunately, its remains were demolished to make way for an extension to the churchyard in 1869.

Peace gradually returned but a period of economic decline also seems to have reduced the town to a very low ebb. Various factors helped Rothbury to recover, including the coming of the railway in 1870 – leading to the opening of an important cattle market and also encouraging the development of the town as a tourist health resort. Lord Armstrong, the wealthy industrialist, also poured money into the redevelopment of the town, giving it the smart Victorian appearance that it still retains today.

St. Oswald's Way leaves Rothbury at the end of the Rothbury Bridge, across the river from the centre of the village.

Sharp's Folly

1 At the bridge, head uphill on the small lane away from the river. At the top of the slope, head straight on then go through a gate into a field. Bear right on the path across the field and up to meet a road junction. Turn left at the road and head to the small settlement of Whitton.

2 Turn off along the second track to the right. Follow the track past Sharp's Folly and onwards for another ½ mile. Turn left at the track junction and head along to Whittondean. Pass to the right of the farmhouse, then turn right along a path with hills in the distance. Follow the waymarked path through to a gate and stile.

Sharp's Folly

Sharp's Folly was built in around 1720 by the then Vicar of Rothbury, Archdeacon Sharp, in the grounds of Whitton Park. It is said to have been built to help overcome local unemployment – an early job-creation project. However, it was also an observatory for the use of the archdeacon who had an interest in astronomy.

3 The path enters rough, hilly ground and also Northumberland National Park at this point. Follow the path uphill to the fascinating archaeological site of Lordenshaws. From the hill there are superb views of the Simonside Hills, the Coquet valley, the distant Cheviot Hills and back towards the coast. An example of cup and ring-marked rocks can be seen over to the right of the main path. Follow the path ahead and downhill to Lordenshaws car park.

Cup and ring-marked rock at Lordenshaws

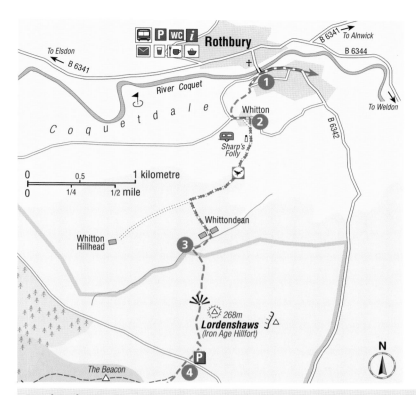

Lordenshaws

The area around Lordenshaws has archaeological features of many ages. The most prominent feature is the Iron Age hill fort that was built at least 2,500 years ago. Northumberland has the largest concentration of these structures in England although here they are generally quite small. They were probably fortified farmsteads that sheltered no more than 100 people. The Lordenshaws fort has, like many in Northumberland, quite elaborate defences. Two new houses were built within the ditched enclosure during Roman times.

Of an earlier date are the cup and ring marks. These are ancient carvings of the Neolithic period and possibly as much as 5,000 years old. They can be found at a number of sites throughout Northumberland and usually take the form of a cup-shaped depression surrounded by circles and grooves. The meaning of this rock art is a matter for speculation. Many of them are to be found carved on stones that command views over a wide area. This is the case with the Lordenshaws carvings, which are among the best to be found.

4 From the Lordenshaws car park, cross the road to the footpath opposite. Follow the path uphill, ignoring paths to the right that head towards The Beacon and the other Simonside Hills. Continue along the waymarked path across the moors and Caudhole Moss. After reaching

the tree plantation, go through a gate and follow the path around to the left of Spylaw Cottage.

Simonside Hills

The Simonside Hills are designated as a Site of Special Scientific Interest (SSSI) and a Special Area of Conservation (SAC) highlighting the area as both nationally and internationally important for wildlife. This area is important for the heather moorland and blanket bog habitats that are found here.

Heather moorland has developed over time as a result of human activity. Areas of woodland were gradually cleared over thousands of years for timber and to allow grazing of stock. Grazing prevents tree regrowth and extensive areas of dwarf shrub (heathers, bilberry etc.) develop. Heather burning provides fresh shoots for sheep and grouse to eat and maintains areas of varied length heather.

Blanket bog, such as at Caudhole Moss, forms where conditions are cool and wet and where bog mosses (sphagnum) and other bog plants flourish. When the sphagnum mosses die, the waterlogged conditions mean they do not break down fully and remain partially decomposed and build up to form peat. These layers of peat build up over time and in places on the Simonside Hills may exceed 15 metres in depth.

Species that may be seen include red grouse, roe deer, skylarks, meadow pipits, wheatears, sphagnum, heather – both ling and bell heather, bilberry, crowberry and bog plants such as cotton grass, bog asphodel and sundews. Rarer species that may be found in the area include red squirrels in the conifer blocks and ravens and peregrines around the crags.

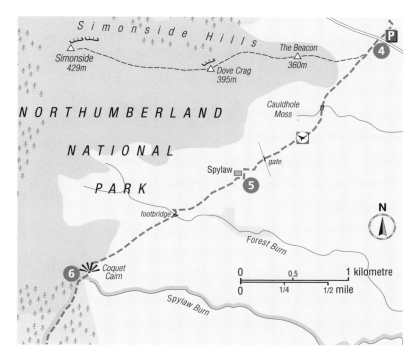

5 The footpath then runs across rough grazing land and more moorland to reach a footbridge across Forest Burn. Follow the track away from the burn, with the Simonside Hills behind you. The route then continues along a footpath crossing the moor, rising slowly uphill towards a large conifer plantation. You eventually reach Coquet Cairn, the highest point of St. Oswald's Way, with good views of hills, moorland and, on a clear day, back to the North Sea.

6 Cross the stile and enter Harwood Forest. Follow the bridleway through the trees until reaching a stone forestry track. Turn left and follow the track for ¼ mile. After crossing a bridge, walk uphill for a short distance, then leave the track on a path to the right. Walk up the path, cross the stone track and go straight ahead into a plantation.

7 Follow the narrow path through the trees until you reach a dry stone wall. Turn right and follow the path along the wall and across to a forestry track. Turn left towards Fallowlees farmhouse, then

Fallowlees

follow the track around to the right. Continue along the track for ¾ mile then, on a right-hand bend, turn left onto a footpath.

Harwood Forest

Harwood Forest, planted predominantly in the 1950s by the Forestry Commission, is a 3,500 hectares (13½ square miles) woodland. The original crop was planted to provide a strategic reserve for the country following the Second World War. Since the 1990s the forest has started to see a lot of changes with a number of areas being felled. The uneven age structure that is created provides a diverse habitat for a wide variety of wildlife. It also allows distant views both within and to the outside of the woodland.

The areas close to the streams are also being managed to create open broadleaf woodland. This creates an ideal habitat for encouraging the passage of wild animals through the area. While walking through, keep a look out for roe deer, red squirrels, raptors, crossbills, siskins and many smaller songbirds.

This is a working forest, so keep a look out for current activities and observe all warning signs.

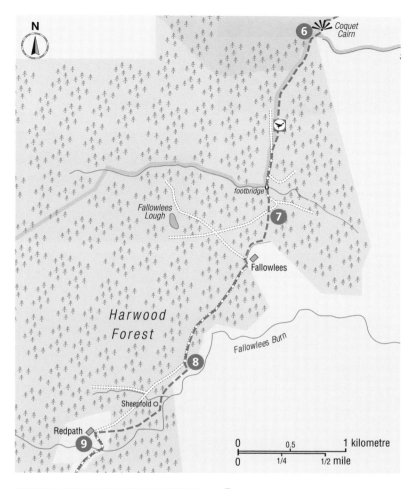

N

Coquet
Cairn

footbridge

Fallowlees
Lough

Fallowlees

Harwood
Forest

Fallowlees Burn

Sheepfold

Redpath

0	0,5	1 kilometre
0	1/4	1/2 mile

8 Follow the path to a stile, cross the corner of a field and head back towards the forest. Turn left to cross a stream and along a path. Pass the remains of a sheepfold and continue along a wide path for about 400 yards, before turning right onto a narrow path into a more open woodland. Follow the winding path through the trees to a gate, then cross the rough field to the old farmhouse of Redpath.

Redpath

9 Turn left along the forestry track, past the open fields and back into the forest. When reaching a T-junction, turn left and follow the track down into the small settlement of Harwood.

10 Turn right at the junction and walk ahead along the lane until you meet a more major road. Turn left and follow the road for 1/4 mile. Turn right on a footpath and cross the field. Head for a gate on the right-hand side of the field.

11 Go through the gate and follow the path, across the stream and up around to the left. Pass to the right of some trees then turn right before a gate into a farmyard. Follow the path around, turning right then left and keeping the field boundaries on your left-hand side. Pass one tree plantation on your right, then go straight ahead with another plantation on your left.

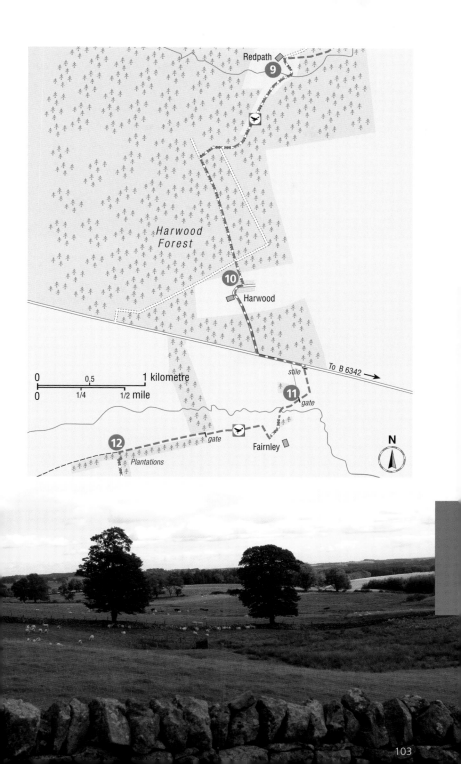

Redpath

9

Harwood
Forest

10

Harwood

To B 6342 →

stile

11

gate

0   0.5   1 kilometre
0   1/4   1/2 mile

gate

12

Fairnley

Plantations

N

12 After 1/2 mile, turn left on a footpath between plantations. Go through a gate then turn right, then left and walk along a track with another plantation on your left-hand side. The track ends at the farm of Catcherside.

13 Turn left at the end and follow the roadway around to the right and through a gateway towards the farmhouse. Before the farmhouse, turn left on the bridleway and go through the right-hand of the two gateways. Follow the bridleway straight ahead and along the left-hand edge of the field.

Catcherside

Bear right at the end of the field and follow the boundary to a gate. Follow the path through to another gateway.

Catcherside

Catcherside Cottage is, in origin, a bastle probably built in the late 16th century. Bastles were rectangular, defensible houses with a barn below and living accommodation above and were built with three-feet thick walls. This design helped protect a family and their livestock from the border raiders or 'reivers' who were common at the time. The building was altered to a cottage in the early 19th century.

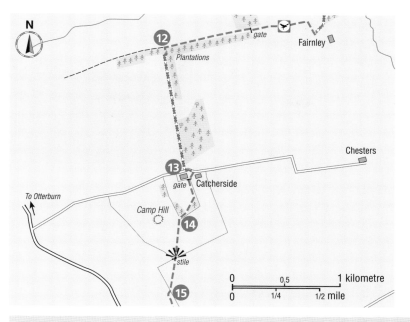

Camp Hill

Between 2,000 and 3,000 years ago, during the Iron Age, people lived in the defended settlement or hill fort at Camp Hill, surrounded by a ditch and rampart. 'Cord rig' earthworks can be seen outside the settlement. Cord rig is a series of narrow ridges generally less than a metre apart, formed as a result of cultivation in the pre-Roman Iron Age.

14 When entering the next field, bear left on a public footpath, with Camp Hill to your right. Go across the rough field, crossing a ditch, then heading to the top of the small hill to reach a stile in the corner of the field, with lovely all-round views of the Northumberland landscape. Cross the next field to another stile.

15 Bear left across the next field and follow the path, through a gap in a wall and around to the left of a conifer plantation. After going through a gate onto a track, turn right (along the line of an old railway), then left between the houses to meet the road at the settlement of Knowesgate.

Wansbeck Valley Railway

The Wansbeck Valley Railway (known locally as 'The Wannie Line') was built between 1862 and 1865. It ran from Morpeth to Redesdale, where it joined the Border County Railway line from Hexham to Hawick. There was a station at Knowesgate.

16 Turn left and walk along the road for 200 yards, then turn right up the driveway to West Whitehill. Pass the farmhouse and follow the bridleway through some gates. Follow the line of earthworks down through the field, with views, on a clear day, of the distant Pennine Hills. At the bottom of the field, cross over a stile on the right-hand side, onto the road verge.

Earthworks north of Kirkwhelpington

Between West Whitehill and the village of Kirkwhelpington, there are a number of ridges and hollows in the fields. These have been made in a variety of ways, including for a medieval field system. There is also a series of 'hollow ways' that appear to lead towards the village. They have steep sides and are thought to have been created by the movement of packhorses and livestock. They were probably part of a droving route between England and Scotland.

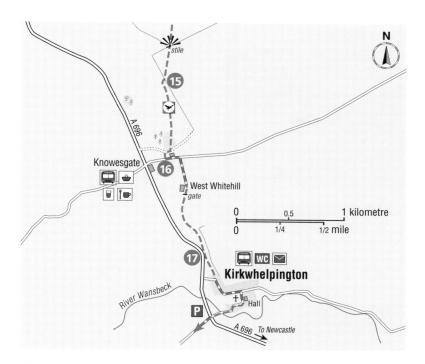

17 Walk along the verge for a few yards, then leave the road at a stile and follow a footpath on the left-hand side. Follow the path straight ahead to the edge of Kirkwhelpington. Go straight on at the road, around to the left, then turn right to the centre of the village and the Memorial Hall.

Earthworks north of Kirkwhelpington

Kirkwhelpington

The name 'Whelpington' begins to appear in documents in the medieval period. During this time there was a village at West Whelpington, which had at least 25 houses. The tenants were all evicted in 1720 in the name of more modern agricultural practices. The remains of the village are perched on the edge of a whinstone quarry, now used as a police firing range.

The present St. Bartholomew's Church in Kirkwhelpington was built in the 13th century, with the first recorded vicar being Walter Crespyn in 1244. It was originally a larger building, with aisles and transepts.

The parish took a long time to recover from the border troubles during the 16th and 17th centuries. Restoration work was carried out on the church during the 18th century and the oldest gravestones in the churchyard date from this time. (One of the most interesting modern graves is that of Sir Charles Parsons (1854-1931), the inventor of the steam turbine, who lived nearby.) In 1760 the vicar's tower or pele was altered and extended. The Rev. John Hodgson lived here between 1823 and 1832 when he wrote most of his classic 'History of Northumberland'.

The rest of the village was made of simple, heather-thatched, two-roomed dwellings until the 1850s, when the stone built, slate roofed cottages, which now characterise the village, began to be built. Many of the purpose built buildings are now private dwellings. The

grey stone courthouse was built in 1851 with the large courtroom taking up the first floor and the policeman's house and prison cells on the ground floor. The school was built in 1858 by public subscription but closed in 1972. Overlooking the village green was The Board Inn. After a petition by wives of the village in 1916, the inn was changed to a temperance hotel. The old blacksmith's house and smithy are at the end of the village green.

The bridge over the River Wansbeck was erected by voluntary subscription and labour in 1818. The date on the bridge was moved to the outside during later repair work.

Hadrian's Wall Path

Hadrian's Wall Path National Trail runs over archaeological earthworks that are of international significance. In 2005 UNESCO included Hadrian's Wall in the new pan-European 'Frontiers of the Roman Empire World Heritage Site'.

The best way to protect any buried archaeology is to ensure that the path remains as a natural grass surface. The Trail is not promoted as a walk during the wet winter months (November to April) when the soils are waterlogged and the risk of erosion is greatest. Please, therefore, try to avoid using the Trail section of St. Oswald's Way during this period (see www.nationaltrail.co.uk/hadrianswall for further advice).

Distances from Kirkwhelpington to:

Great Whittington
10½ miles (17 km)

Heavenfield
17½ miles (28½ km)

St. Oswald's Way

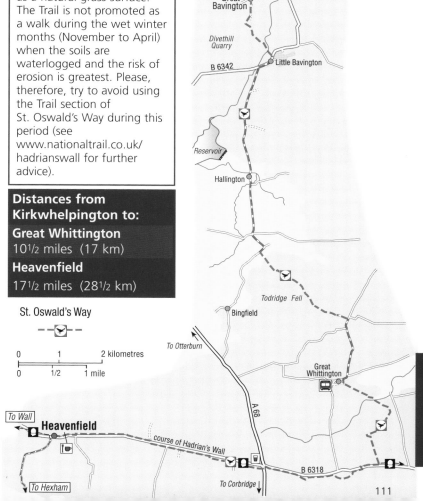

0   1   2 kilometres

0   1/2   1 mile

1 From the Memorial Hall at Kirkwhelpington, follow the road between the Church of St. Bartholomew and the village green. Cross the River Wansbeck and meet the A696.

2 Carefully cross the main road and go straight ahead along a narrow lane. Follow the road as it bends to the left then the right, then turn left on the path just before the farm buildings. Go straight on along the path, crossing the field to meet another lane.

3 Turn right and follow the lane, ignoring the turn-off to the right, to reach West Harle. Pass the farm buildings to the left, then turn right along an old track.

West Harle

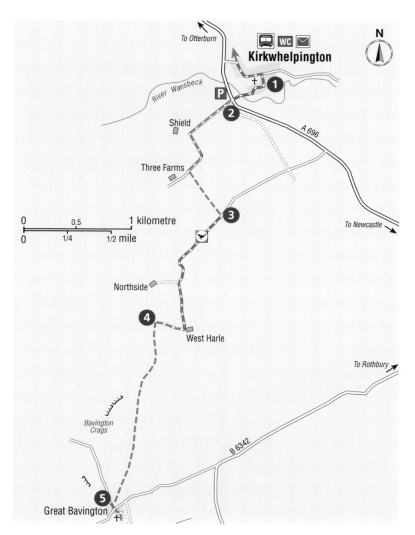

4 After 300 yards, turn left through a gate and then walk with the field boundary on your left. Bear right at the bottom of the field and cross a stile. Follow the path ahead towards some of the Bavington Crags, then bear left up the hill to another stile. Go straight on along the path and follow it ahead, to reach the small village of Great Bavington.

Bavington Crags

Bavington Crags, and those to the south of Great Bavington are further outcrops of the Whin Sill. The crags near to the village have been designated as a Site of Special Scientific Interest, as they support a distinctive range of plants, featuring several nationally uncommon species, which is found at only a small number of other sites on the Whin Sill in Northumberland.

The nearby Divetill Quarry began operations in 1934 and is still in use. The quarried whinstone is processed and coated for roadstone products.

Great Bavington

5 After joining the road in the village, bear left onto an old track that runs between houses and around to the right past the United Reformed Church. Follow the route through to meet a driveway that leads towards a farm. About 200 yards before the buildings, bear right over a stile and across a field. Cross the next stile and follow the path through a small plantation.

Great Bavington

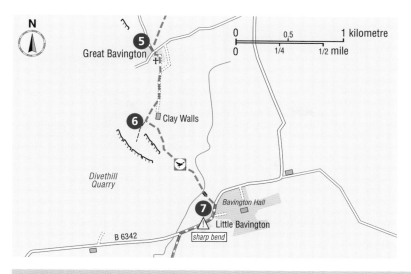

Great Bavington

Although it is now a very small, quiet village, Great Bavington used to be much larger. The village probably reduced in size due to outbreaks of the plague and poor harvests in the 14th century.

The oldest building now standing in the village was built in 1625 and was once a pub called the Harvest Home. Next door is what was the village school, with a Victorian postbox in the wall. After the school closed, it became a popular youth hostel but this was closed due to the 'unseemly behaviour' of the hostellers.

The nearby church was built in 1725 and is the third oldest Presbyterian congregation in England.

6 Turn left after the plantation then follow the waymarked path to the right of the farmhouse, past a field corner, then down the field on the right-hand side of an old dry stone wall. At the bottom of the field, bear right past a small plantation, then bear slightly left across the next field to a small gate. Go straight ahead along a line of trees to reach a stile at a road in Little Bavington.

Little Bavington

Little Bavington is another settlement with a long history. Evidence of a deserted medieval village has been found and there are records of a chapel in the 13th century and a possible tower in later years.

Bavington Hall, in the park to the east of Little Bavington, is a solid and sizable stone house built in the late 17th century, probably for Admiral George Delaval. It has since been altered, extended and repaired. It used to stand in large-scale 18th century landscaped gardens, although little of these now remains.

7 Cross the road when safe to do so and turn right, walking around the outside of the sharp right-hand bend ahead. About 200 yards after the bend, turn left along a lane. Dovecote Hill can be seen to the right from this lane. Continue straight on to eventually reach the small settlement of Hallington.

Dovecote Hill

To the west of Little Bavington, on a small hill, is the most significant remainder of the landscaped gardens of Bavington Hall. This was built as an 'eyecatcher' and to look like a miniature castle. It may have been a dovecote as well as a focal point.

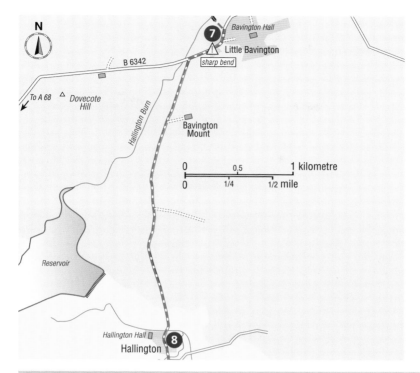

Hallington

The four reservoirs in the Hallington area were built by the Newcastle and Gateshead Water Company to supply water to Tyneside. East Hallington, with a capacity of 685 million gallons (3.1 million cubic metres), was completed in 1872. A number of geological problems had to be overcome in the construction of the 1,068 million gallon Colt Crag Reservoir which came into use in 1884. The much smaller Little Swinburn was completed in 1879 and the fourth, West Hallington, followed shortly afterwards. Hallington Hall was built for Ralph Soulby in 1768. Alterations and additions were made in the late 18th and mid 19th centuries for the subsequent owners, the Trevelyans. A Roman altar and a dovecote stand in the grounds of the Hall.

8 Continue ahead along the lane for another mile until reaching a crossroads. Cross carefully and go straight ahead past the war memorial. Follow the road around to the right at the top of the hill, then turn left onto a bridleway a little further on. Follow the bridleway ahead, along the edges of fields.

Hallington

9 Go through a small gate into a rougher field then walk uphill with a wall on your right-hand side, to a gate at the top of the field. There are excellent views to the north from this point.

10 After going through the gate, go straight ahead across the next field. At the next gate, bear left towards another gate in the far corner of the field, passing the highest point of Todridge Fell to your right. Lovely views across the Tyne valley to the Pennines can be see to the south on a clear day. Walk along the edge of the next field for about 100 yards, to a small gate on your left.

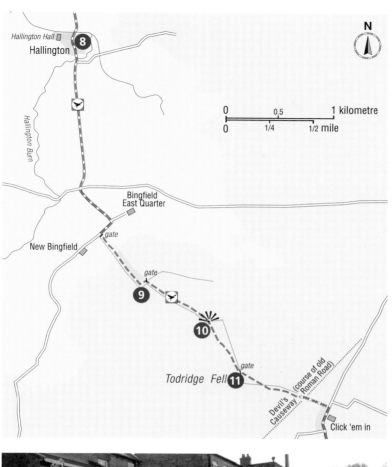

Hallington Hall
Hallington **8**

Hallington Burn

0   0.5   1 kilometre
0   1/4   1/2 mile

N

Bingfield
East Quarter

gate

New Bingfield

gate

9

10

Todridge Fell *gate* **11** (course of old Roman Road)

Devil's Causeway

Click 'em in

*Great
Whittington*

Great Whittington

11 Go through the gate and hedge, then bear right across the field. Walk near to a stream on your right to reach another gate. Go through the gate and turn left along the edge of the field. Follow the path straight ahead, crossing the course of the Devil's Causeway, to reach the road at Click 'Em In. Turn right at the road and, ignoring roads on the right then the left, follow it through to the village of Great Whittington.

Great Whittington

This is a pleasant small village with numerous stone houses, many of them built in the early 19th century. The village has a small Methodist Chapel (now a private house) that was built in 1835 and a thriving agricultural engineering business. It is probably the site of a deserted medieval village.

12 Just before the Queen's Head, turn left onto a track. At the bend ahead, turn left through a gate, then bear left through another gate. Follow the path, crossing a ditch then straight ahead towards a gate and stile. Cross the stile and walk up the right-hand side of the field to an old windmill.

13 Cross the boundary at the windmill. Please note that the path from here may become diverted to provide a more direct route over Toft Hill to point 15. Please make sure that you follow the waymarking. Otherwise, follow the path through the buildings ahead. At the buildings, go straight ahead and through to a field. Bear left across the field to a stile. Bear right across the next field to another stile, then straight uphill to the right of some pens at Clarewood.

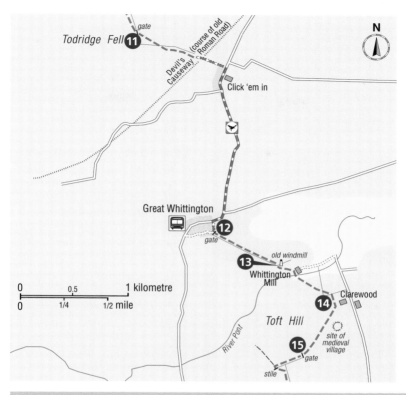

Whittington Mill

Whittington windmill is a round stone building and was probably constructed in the 18th century. Only the walls of the mill now survive as the sails and roof blew off in 1900. Close to the windmill is an 18th century, three-storey watermill – the west gable used to house the wheel. This site has probably been home to a watermill since medieval times.

14 Pass the pens, then go through a gate on the right. Head uphill, passing the site of Clarewood medieval village, diagonally across the field to reach a kissing gate. Go through the gate and bear slightly left across the next field to a small gate on the far side.

Clarewood Medieval Village

Clarewood was known to exist in 1296 but most of the inhabitants were thought to have left in the late 17th century. The remains of several areas of ridge and furrow can be seen – this is the result of a method of cultivation that was used throughout the medieval period and later. By the mid 19th century, there were only three farms here.

15 Go through the gate and walk along the left-hand edge of the field to a gate and then a ladder stile. Cross the stile into another field. Bear left across the corner of the field, then walk along the field-edge to meet a road.

The Military Road

The Military Road was built in the 18th century. Its origins lay in 1745 when the English army stationed in Newcastle was unable to reach Carlisle to intercept the invading Scottish army led by Bonnie Prince Charlie. The road that the English army had to follow was too near the Tyne valley, so a new road on higher ground was the answer. The road was built by General Wade almost exactly on the line of Hadrian's Wall and, since it used the Roman stones as a foundation, frequently on top of it.

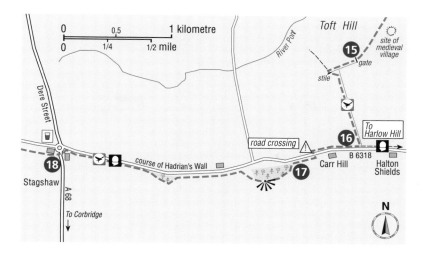

16 At the road, St. Oswald's Way joins Hadrian's Wall Path National Trail and, for the rest of the route, is waymarked with the acorn symbol used for all National Trails. Turn right and follow the path alongside the road. After Carr Hill farm, the route crosses to the other side of the road, then follows the edges of fields on the

other side of a wall. In this area, some of the earthworks of Hadrian's Wall can be seen, with the Vallum in the field to the left and the North Ditch across the road to the right.

Hadrian's Wall Earthworks

17 Head around the left-hand side of the trees on top of a small hill and towards the Vallum, with good views of the Tyne valley. Cut back down to the road at a stile in the corner of the field. Follow the path, parallel to the road, until the A68 at Stagshaw.

Hadrian's Wall

The Roman Emperor Hadrian visited Britain in 122 and it is thought that he ordered the wall to be built at that time. It was built in the following six years by the Roman army, although modifications were still being carried out when Hadrian died in 138. The wall was not essentially a defensive structure: its main purpose was frontier control, guarding the Roman Empire to the south. As first planned, there were gates every Roman mile with small guard posts (milecastles). Portgate, where the present A68 crosses the wall, was one of the milecastles although unusual as one of only two points where a major Roman road (Dere Street) crosses the wall. There are the sites of five mileposts along St. Oswald's Way.

However, the Roman frontier was not just a wall. To the north there was usually a ditch to make the wall more defensible and, to the south, an earthwork known as the Vallum. The Vallum stretched almost the whole length of the wall and was a flat-bottomed ditch (about 20 feet wide and 10 feet deep) with a mound, set back by 30 feet, on either side. Opinions vary as to the purpose of the Vallum: some historians believe it to have marked the southern side of a 'military zone' behind the wall, while others think that it may have been a communication route.

18 At the roundabout, head around to the left and cross the A68 to the left of the Errington Arms. Go through the car park and follow the path through the fields, with the Military Road over to the right.

19 After leaving the trees of Stanley Plantation and crossing a side-road, the route goes through more fields before crossing the road again near Errington Hill Head. Cross carefully then follow the path through the fields to the right of the road. After 1¼ miles, pass St. Oswald's Hill Head Farm and through to the large wooden cross at Heavenfield, the end of St. Oswald's Way.

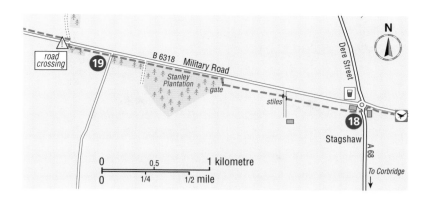

Stagshaw Fair

Stagshaw Bank, to the south of Hadrian's Wall, was once famous for its livestock fairs. Thousands of cattle, sheep and horses were brought to these markets, which attracted people from all over northern England and southern Scotland. Each fair lasted for a week or more and was a spectacular event, full of people and animals.

Stagshaw Fair was hugely important in the Middle Ages for trade in goods as well as livestock. It is thought that the fairs could have had much earlier origins, and they certainly survived for many centuries. Armstrong's map of 1769 marks Stagshaw Bank as the site of "two of the greatest fairs in England".

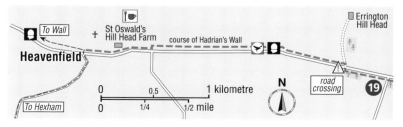

Heavenfield

Oswald's uncle, Edwin, had killed Oswald's father, King Aethelfrith to reign in Northumbria. However, in 633 he was killed in a battle against Cadwallon, the King of Gwynedd, and Penda of Mercia. For a while, Oswald's elder step-brother Eanfrith was king, until he too was killed by Cadwallon.

Oswald had returned to Bernicia from exile when Edwin was killed. It was then that Oswald marched south with a small army to Heavenfield to confront Cadwallon, "the accursed leader of the Britons and all that vast army that he boasted none could resist".

The Battle of Heavenfield took place in around 634. The night before the battle, Oswald and his men were stationed here and built and erected a large wooden cross on the high ground and prayed to God for success in their fight.

It is not clear from historical records where the battle took place, but tradition has it that a large number of skulls and sword hilts have been uncovered in a field known as Mould's Close on the south side of the road. It is thought that Cadwallon himself was killed on the banks of Rowley Burn, about seven miles to the south of here.

Monks from the abbey at Hexham held an annual pilgrimage to Heavenfield and to the wooden cross. Splinters of wood from the cross were believed to be the cause of miracles and the site became so popular that a small church was built here in the late 7th century. The present St. Oswald's Church is probably the third on the site and was built in the 18th century. An annual pilgrimage from Hexham to Heavenfield is still held, on or around St. Oswald's Day (5th August).

The large wooden cross now standing at Heavenfield was erected by a group of local people in 1927, replacing a stone cross that had stood here until 1807. The stone cross used a Roman altar as its base stone and the altar is now in St. Oswald's Church.

Distances from Heavenfield to:

Wall
1 1/2 miles   (2 1/2 km)

Hexham
4 miles   (6 1/2 km)

Unfortunately there is no public transport to Heavenfield and no suitable car parking. Therefore, you are advised to continue walking along Hadrian's Wall Path to the village of Wall, or head south into Hexham.

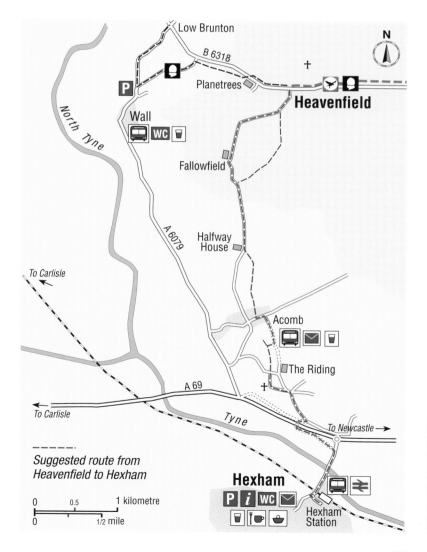

Suggested route from Heavenfield to Hexham

USEFUL CONTACTS

St. Oswald's Way
Web: www.stoswaldsway.com

Alnwick District Council
Tel: 01665 510505
Email: customerservices@alnwick.gov.uk
Web: www.alnwick.gov.uk

Northumberland County Council
Tel: 01670 533000
Email: customerservices@northumberland.gov.uk
Web: www.northumberland.gov.uk

Northumberland National Park Authority:
Tel: 01434 605555
Email: enquiries@nnpa.org.uk
Web: www.northumberland-national-park.org.uk

Northumberland Coast AONB Partnership
Tel: 01670 534088
Email: CoastAONB@Northumberland.gov.uk
Web: www.northumberlandcoastaonb.org

Traveline (for public transport information)
Tel: 0870 608 2 608
Web: www.traveline.org.uk

Northumberland Tourism
Tel: 01670 794520
Web: www.visitnorthumberland.com

One North East Tourism Team
Tel: 0191 229 6200
Web: www.visitnortheastengland.com

Hadrian's Wall Path
Web: www.nationaltrail.co.uk/hadrianswall

North Sea Trail
Web: www.northseatrail.org